COOL SUCCESS

Cool Success

Navigating the Highs and Lows of HVAC & Life

Brandon Brown

To Dara, Parker, Dawson, Mom, Dad, and all my employees and customers.

Table of Contents

Introduction

In a world filled with stories of rags to riches, tales of ordinary individuals who defy the odds and achieve extraordinary success captivate our hearts and inspire us to reach for our own dreams. Such is the story of Brandon Brown, whose remarkable journey from humble beginnings to triumph is a testament to the power of faith, service, and determination.

"Cool Success" takes us on an immersive expedition through the life of Brandon—a small-town boy who, like many of us, dared to dream big—while honoring the transformative power of his experiences, the pivotal role of his faith, and the countless, often-times hard-learned lessons acquired along the way.

Chapter by chapter, we are invited to accompany Brandon on his odyssey, beginning with his upbringing in the small town of Concord, VA. Rooted in a Christian home, his formative years instilled in him a strong sense of faith, family, and community. We witness the impact of these early influences as he discovers a passion for service, devoting himself to helping others through church activities and volunteer work.

As Brandon traverses the path of self-discovery, a new direction in his life emerges. He delves into vocational options during high school, ultimately choosing to pursue a career in HVAC, which serves as the foundation for his future endeavors. The delicate balance between education and hands-on experience was equally pivotal in transforming distant dreams into a tangible reality—a reality more within his grasp than he'd thought.

From his early days as a technician to his eventual rise as a lead service technician at the age of 20, Brandon grapples with questions about the meaning and impact of his chosen profession. However, it is a decisive moment during the aftermath of Hurricane Katrina that ignites a flame within him—a call to serve that leads him to join FEMA as a volunteer firefighter. The challenges faced during this time, including balancing work responsibilities and the desire to help others, became the crucible in which his entrepreneurial spirit was forged.

It is during the subsequent chapter that we witness the birth of an entrepreneur. Encouraged by his wife, Brandon takes the courageous leap into starting his own HVAC business. In the face of initial struggles and the daunting task of establishing a unique identity in a competitive market, he navigates the treacherous waters of entrepreneurship with resilience, determination, and—the most important ingredient—strong core values rooted in service. This chapter not only offers insights into infiltrating a new market but also delves into the 2008/2009 real estate market crash, illuminating the extensive impact it had on his journey.

The subsequent chapters chronicle the challenges, triumphs, and growth that Brandon experiences as he scales up his business, learns to lead, and reflects on the journey he has undertaken. We witness the delicate balance he strikes between firefighting and business ownership, the thrill of securing significant contracts, and the development of his leadership skills. Through it all, Brandon maintains a resolute faith and trust in God's plan—barring some natural doubts in moments of desolation—providing a guiding light even in the darkest of times.

"Cool Success" culminates in a reflection on the profound lessons learned throughout the journey. Brandon imparts invaluable insights for aspiring entrepreneurs and individuals seeking fulfillment in their careers. With unwavering honesty, he shares the joys and tribulations, the risks and rewards, and the ultimate satisfaction of finding purpose and making a difference.

Chapter 1: Growing Up in Concord, VA

If you had asked me during my childhood whether I saw myself in a leadership role, I would have eagerly agreed, even if I didn't know what exactly that would entail. All I knew, even before my cognition had fully developed, is that a leader is one who serves, and service was what came naturally to me—it was encoded into my body and my soul. However, if you had suggested that I would one day sit down and chronicle my journey for the scrutiny of the public eye, I would have chuckled and dismissed the very idea. Imagine—someone reads my life story and actually gets something out of it? Is my story even worth telling? Imagine… yet here I am. And as I sit here today, recounting and reminiscing over days past, a sense of hope and anticipation fills my heart. I recognize that my experiences and insights may pale in comparison to the extraordinary figures that have shaped history. However, I believe that within the tapestry of my own story, there lies a universal thread that can resonate with anyone who has ever taken a leap of faith (or multiple if you're anything like me and don't mind falling flat on your face sometimes).

Growing up in the small town of Concord, Virginia, I was blessed with a childhood filled with love, simplicity, and a strong sense of community. Nestled amidst the rolling hills and serene landscapes, Concord was the kind of town where everyone knew one another and life moved at a gentle pace. I was blessed to be raised in a place that perfectly complemented my temperament and nurtured my disposition to serve my community. With its close-knit community combined with my overly-friendly disposition, Concord provided a fertile ground for relationships to flourish. Neighbors were not merely neighbors; they were extended family members. We celebrated each other's triumphs, supported one another in times of need, and shared in the simplest pleasures that life had to offer. Some of my fondest memories of my hometown are woven by the grand spectacle of the annual Fourth of July parade hosted by Concord for over half a century. Attendance in the parade was not just a casual affair but a revered family tradition that left no room for exceptions. In fact, it seemed as though the entire community adhered to this unspoken rule, as the parade drew in participation from the whole community, including the fire department, local farmers, churches, and sports teams, inevitably giving rise to an atmosphere brimming with unity and camaraderie. However, the true highlight for me came after the parade at the post-parade after-party. Well, calling it a mere "party" would be an understatement; it was more akin to a festival. Once the procession concluded, our entire community converged at the local volunteer fire department, indulging in delectable food and engaging in a myriad of exciting games. Indeed, there was always an undeniable spirit of camaraderie that permeated every aspect of our lives.

At the center of my world were my parents, Randy and Joanne, who instilled in me the values of honesty, compassion, and hard work. They were the pillars of strength and guidance in my life, never failing to provide a nurturing environment that allowed me to grow and discover my true potential, even though they themselves knew it all along. All throughout my childhood, my parents had this unwavering belief that I would grow up to be involved in either business or leadership. They fondly recount a particular incident from when I was around six or seven years old, which serves as a testament to their conviction in me. It was just an ordinary day at home—my father was off at work, and my mother decided to take a quick shower while my three siblings and I kept ourselves entertained. There was a knock on our front door, and I went to answer it—it was a vacuum salesman who had come to demonstrate his product. Without hesitation, I welcomed him in. What else could I have done? Here, on my front steps, was a hardworking man out making an honest living, and even six-year-old Brandon knew that he was deserving of respect. My parents, however, were oblivious to the surprise that awaited them. Picture this: my mother, with nothing but a towel wrapped around her, comes out of the shower and steps into the living room, expecting to find her children innocently playing. Instead, she discovers me enthusiastically assisting this random salesman in setting up his presentation. Startled, she hurriedly retreated to her room to get dressed, and by the time she had returned and the salesman and me—his assistant—had finished setting up the presentation, both she and my dad felt compelled to sit through the entire presentation out of courtesy. I don't quite recall if we ended up purchasing a vacuum that day, but what I do remember is the sheer joy I felt in being the salesman's trusted assistant during the setup. I might even have been the best assistant he had ever had.

My parents, though mildly annoyed at my antics, earn full credit for them; they are the ones who instilled in me a strong work ethic and a profound respect for people who put in the effort. They worked tirelessly and would often work multiple jobs to provide for a large household consisting of five children: me, my sister, and my three brothers. With so many kids to look after, my parents ingeniously crafted a solution that would not only allow my mom to work from the comfort of our own home but also provide socialization for their own children. My mother, with her deep-rooted maternal instincts, started a home-based daycare and preschool. Our humble abode transformed into a vibrant hub, welcoming laughter and the pitter-patter of tiny feet, filling our days with endless joy and companionship. Summertime, in particular, was always an adventure of epic proportions; with so many kids around, my siblings and I were never bored. There was always a new friend to join our escapades.

Cool Success

Meanwhile, my father was equally committed to providing for our family, and his journey from truck driver and security guard to Security Supervisor was a true testament to his character, unwavering work ethic, and genuine concern for the safety and well-being of others—the same qualities that I am grateful for being instilled in me. Before the sun had risen, he would set out on his route as a dedicated truck driver, transporting goods for a local company. From the early morning hours until late into the evening, he traversed the roads, ensuring deliveries reached their destinations without fail. But his dedication didn't end there. Beyond his role as a truck driver, he took on the responsibility of a security guard for local department stores, dedicated to preserving the peace within their walls. To many, the role of a security guard may seem like a menial job. But for my father, and by extension me, this was one of the most important jobs out there, and he took it seriously. As such, after years of perseverance, my father's steadfast dedication led him to a pivotal moment in his career. He secured a coveted position as a Security Supervisor at the local hospital—a role that would define his professional journey until retirement.

Then, there were my siblings. I have an older sister with whom I had a functioning relationship; I loved her, of course, but given that she was older than me by seven years, our differing outlooks on and experiences in life led us down very different paths from the get-go. I also have three younger brothers. Being the oldest brother certainly comes with its fair share of responsibilities, which I was more than happy to fulfill. Growing up, my brothers and I were incredibly close, barring our naturally different personalities, friend groups, and hobbies, and I always felt very protective over them. I would love to sit here and write that that level of closeness and involvement in each other's lives withstood the test of time, but alas, it did not. What did last to date, however, was the bond, love, and profound respect and pride we carried for each other. Despite the logistics being stacked against their favor, my parents always made sure each of us had what we needed: food, clothes, love, laughter, and, most importantly, a strong faith.

Growing up in a Christian home profoundly influenced the way I viewed the world and shaped the person I became. Our family's faith was not merely a Sunday ritual; it was a way of life, and I loved it. I loved all of it—the Sunday morning services, Sunday night bible studies, Wednesday night awanas, and Saturday Youth groups. I count myself truly blessed to grow up how I did, surrounded and guided by faith. I grew up in the embrace of a Baptist Church community, being saved and baptized at 12 years old. The belief in salvation as the pathway to heaven has remained steadfast within my heart. At the same time, though, my faith also instilled in me the belief that every individual, regardless of their religious standing, deserved to be treated with kindness, compassion, and respect. This belief guided my interactions with the community, where I witnessed firsthand the struggles faced by many families, the challenges some children encounter, and the weighty decisions that burdened their young hearts.

For our Youth group, church camp would be the highlight of our summers. It was a spiritual oasis tucked away in the serene mountains of Virginia. For a whole week, it was us kids, our Youth leaders, and the preachers. The days were jam-packed with activities. The sermons and the singing were pretty much a given. But there were also sports, talent shows, and a huge pool for us to splash around in—it was every kid's summer dream. Our favorite part was definitely the final night activities; like a sacred ritual, we would all gather around the crackling bonfire, the atmosphere tinged with both excitement and poignancy. Each of us, holding a stick in our hands, had a chance to stand before the group and share what we treasured most about camp. We would then make a promise—both to ourselves and the group as a kind of public declaration—to do one meaningful thing once we returned home. And then, we would toss our sticks into the dancing flames to symbolize our commitment to fulfill that promise. Yeah, church camps could get intense, and that's exactly what I loved about it. Those final nights at camp were nothing short of transformative. Emotions flowed freely as confessions and pledges filled the air. For every soul in that circle, it was a moment of deep connection with our faith and a reaffirmation of our love for God.

At age 13, I eagerly embraced the opportunity to serve as the awanas game director and bus ministry helper. Every Tuesday evening, alongside other devoted church members, I would venture door-to-door, extending invitations to children and their families, introducing them to the fellowship of our church community, and inviting them to join us for awanas activities. It was an endeavor that captured my youthful enthusiasm, and before long, our bus route brimmed with eager faces each Wednesday night and Sunday morning, ready to be picked up for church. Engaging with children and families from diverse backgrounds spanning various income levels became an integral part of my daily life. Their backgrounds did not matter to me; instead, I always recognized that our shared humanity transcends all material boundaries. Our neighborhood, though small even by the standards of the 80s, boasted an array of diverse households and families from all walks of life. Yet, to me, these differences were never barriers but rather invitations to connect and embrace the beauty of our shared humanity. Love, acceptance, and a genuine fondness for others were the guiding forces that fuelled my interactions, allowing me to see beyond the superficial. I was blessed with an innate ability to connect with anyone I encountered, forming friendships and relishing the opportunity to ensure their participation in church activities. Through it all, I witnessed the power of prayer, the comfort of knowing there was a higher purpose to our existence, and the strength that came from believing in something greater than ourselves. Most of all, it sowed in me the seeds of responsibility, empathy, and compassion.

Our extensive involvement in church activities and regular worship services brought us closer to our community, fostering a deep sense of belonging and shared values. But the most surprising thing was that it all felt very natural to me; thanks to my outgoing nature, I effortlessly forged friendships with people from all walks of life, and my parents can attest to this fact. From the moment I uttered my first words, my parents knew they had a chatterbox on their hands. I seemed to have a natural gift for gab, chatting away even before I took my first wobbly steps. My mom often recalls how I could strike up a conversation with almost anyone, even as a precocious five-year-old. I would be strolling down the grocery store aisles with my parents when, suddenly, I would find myself deep in conversation with a complete stranger, sharing stories and laughter ("stranger danger" wasn't as pervasive in our close-knit community). Stunts like these became predictable patterns in my early years. And though I would call it endearing, you can imagine that my loquacious tendencies didn't always bode well for me in the confines of a classroom. The teachers, bless their patient souls, would often have to remind me to rein in my exuberant chatter. I couldn't resist the urge to share my thoughts, ideas, and, yes, even the more-than-occasional joke. Sorry, teachers! I suppose my zest for communication simply couldn't be contained within the four walls of a classroom. There was an innate joy in forming new connections that resonated deeply within me. From my earliest years, I eagerly embraced church, actively participating in various church activities, and wholeheartedly immersing myself in the vibrant tapestry of service, fellowship, and leadership opportunities— three invaluable pillars that held immense significance in my life from a very young age.

As I look back on those formative years of my upbringing in Concord, VA, I realize how the seeds of service and community were sown in my heart. The experience within my close-knit family, along with the guidance of my parents and God, instilled in me values that, unbeknownst to me, would guide me on a remarkable journey as I transitioned into adolescence. That is when my passion for service truly kindled, and the seeds of purpose finally began to take root. In sharing my story, I am driven by a deep desire to serve, to make a positive impact on the lives of others. The echoes of that little boy, who found joy in assisting a vacuum salesman, still reverberate within me. I can't help but envision someone, just like that younger version of myself, finding solace, inspiration, or guidance within the pages of this book.

Chapter 2: Discovering a Passion for Service

In the crucible of youth, where innocence meets curiosity, a profound awakening was waiting to unfold. For me, in my childhood years, mischief and service danced hand in hand. Amidst my rambunctious adventures, a deeper realization began to brew. Yes, I'll admit it—I was a talker from the get-go; I could chat up a storm before I even knew how to tie my shoelaces, much to my parents' amusement. They would often say that I could strike up a conversation with a brick wall and keep it entertained. It was as though I knew no stranger.

But little did we know that my penchant for gab would soon be put to good use.

From an early age, I discovered that service wasn't just a fleeting interest; it was ingrained in my very DNA—I couldn't escape it if I wanted to. Don't get me wrong; I wasn't born with a little service cape, marked with a life of service and ready to leap into action. My environment definitely had a pivotal role to play. Nature vs nurture—it's the classic debate, and I'd say my calling to serve was a tag-team effort. My environment surrounded me with examples of kindness and compassion, enabling and reinforcing my innate disposition towards service. It just so happened that every path I took seemed to lead me towards opportunities to lend a hand. In that way, I guess you could say service was my destiny, and my journey was merely following the trail of breadcrumbs that life left for me.

Of course, I took a few detours along the way, as one does. One of my earliest failed pursuits was that of a mechanic. As the oldest son, I got the golden ticket to assist my dad around the house with his handyman projects. My dad was Mr. Fix-it, determined to tackle every repair and maintenance task himself, no matter what. From vehicles to lawnmowers to that trusty camper, he was a DIY hero. So, at the ripe age of nine, with a head full of know-how from watching my dad, I decided to take matters into my own hands. Vacation was looming, and we had a hefty to-do list to tackle. I felt like the hero my dad needed, the savior of his pre-vacation frenzy.

Cool Success

But you know how it goes—good intentions pave the way to some of the most comical disasters. I checked the car and found the radiator a tad low. No worries, Dad; I got this! I proudly filled it up with water, patted myself on the back, and thought I was destined to be the next auto expert. Of course, I got side-tracked and forgot to inform my dad of my heroic act. Little did I know that my fate as the family's future mechanic was about to take a tragic turn.

Off went Dad to the store, but 20 minutes later, the phone rang—it was the call of doom. He was stranded at the store, and the car was kaput. What in the world happened? I had checked it over meticulously! We soon discovered the bitter truth: I had filled the wrong compartment! Instead of the radiator, I had pumped water into the oil compartment, and you can probably guess how that ended—a fried engine and my dreams of being the family's mechanical prodigy dashed to pieces. Well, my mechanic career may have been short-lived, but I learned an invaluable lesson—always double-check and never assume you know it all.

But really, my dream wasn't so much becoming a mechanic than it was, I now realize, helping and serving others in any way I can. In contemplating my innate inclination towards service, I am reminded of an intriguing historical account that highlights the essence of human nature. Anthropologists often refer to the famous "femur healing" example to underscore the significance of service and care in human evolution. It is believed that the first signs of "civilization" emerged when early humans began to demonstrate empathy and compassion towards one another.

Imagine a time long ago, when our ancestors roamed the vast savannas, grappling with the harsh realities of survival. Amidst the wild landscapes, they encountered inevitable dangers and faced challenges that could easily lead to injuries and death. During these formidable times, an individual with a broken femur would have been gravely compromised, unable to hunt, gather, or escape danger. Such an injury would have been a severe blow to survival.

However, this is where something remarkable happened— instead of abandoning their injured companion to face a certain fate, evidence suggests that early humans came together to provide assistance. They offered help, care, and support to the wounded member, enabling them to recover and heal. This compassionate act of service displayed the seeds of civilization, the roots of community and cooperation that would lay the foundation for our shared human experience.

From the moment I could grasp the notion of service, something clicked in my still-developing brain: I knew it was my calling in life. It was as if a guiding force within me whispered, "This is what you are meant to do." Call it intuition or God. For me, personally, it was definitely the latter. My soul had indeed been deeply touched within the hallowed walls of the church. My involvement in church activities and worship services since early childhood became a reflection of that same calling to serve. My heart, I learned, was that of a servant.

But this calling to serve was not limited to the confines of one institution or one community.

Now, let's be real here—the service industry can be a wild rollercoaster ride. Learning how to communicate, problem-solve, and find the silver lining for others isn't for the faint of heart. It's like navigating a maze full of colorful characters, each with their quirks and unique ways of handling stress. But you know what? I somehow discovered an innate power—a calming effect that put people at ease and made them trust my guidance. Go figure! Maybe it was my quick wit or my knack for cracking jokes and making people laugh. You know, those comebacks and one-liners seemed to come naturally to me. When I had no other answers, humor was my secret weapon— and hey, it still is!

Back to my early years in the service industry. As soon as I learned how to drive and got my hands on those car keys, I raced to join my local Volunteer Fire Department; it was as though I was drawn by an invisible force. This was not completely out of character for me, though; One Christmas, long before the idea to volunteer at the fire department hadn't even formed, I eagerly asked for and graciously received a fire scanner. From that moment on, it became my constant companion. Tucked securely by my side, I would listen intently to the radio calls, feeling a rush of excitement with every report of units en route to an emergency. The sheer joy of hearing the calls come in, the seamless communication among responders, and the coordinated efforts to save lives and property definitely planted the idea in my head, even if I wasn't aware of it at the time.

Cool Success

Fast forward to me joining the "Second Brigade" at the fire department, a special group comprising high school students like me. Joining the Second Brigade was like stepping into a secret society of teenage heroes. The eight of us were the firefighting dream team, complete with our own van for rescues. With only a handful of eager young minds on the team, we were always on standby to assist whenever a fire call came in during school hours. And believe you me, I took my job very seriously. I would be sitting in the middle of a class when suddenly, the PA system would crackle with the words "Second Brigade Report," it was our Bat-Signal. We would be allowed to leave our desks and, without hesitation, spring into action. Sure, my algebra grades might have suffered, but hey, I was acing the real-world lessons.

The thrill of being part of a team dedicated to helping others ignited an unquenchable fire within me (ironic, I know). Volunteering became my passion, my sanctuary, and my second home. There, amidst the camaraderie of fellow firefighters, I found purpose and fulfillment, running calls and taking classes. The fire department became a second home, and my firefighting family became an integral part of my life.

I still remember that one morning during the first period when we rushed off to battle a hay bale fire. A hundred bales ablaze, threatening the woods and barns—talk about a fiery start to the day! And let me tell you, we fought that fire like warriors, earning the admiration of the older firefighters and the farmers. Who knew hay could be so rebellious?

But, of course, it wasn't all fun and games. In the realm of firefighting, we are often confronted with stark reminders of life's brevity. Our emergency adventures exposed us to the harsh realities of life too early. One such incident remains etched in my mind, not just because of how gruesome it was, but also for its profound impact on my sense of purpose. It was a particularly foggy evening when the distressing call came in—a head-on collision with multiple injuries. The tragic details unfolded slowly; apparently, a car's reckless attempt to pass another resulted in a catastrophic collision. The ill-fated car dared to overtake another on a narrow highway, blissfully unaware of the impending disaster that lay ahead. I suppose that's how it goes; you never know which split-second decision is going to be your final, and as much as we would all love to point fingers at the overtaking car, the truth is, we are all guilty of such actions at some point. It's nothing but sheer luck, or perhaps the graceful watch of a higher power that protects us from similar fates every waking, unsuspecting hour of our lives. So, as the car switched lanes, an oncoming car approached from the opposite direction, and the two vehicles met with a cataclysmic force. The gravity of the situation became painfully clear as we first assessed the scene, knowing full well it would be a difficult sight to forget. Upon seeing the wreckage, I could almost hear the deafening sound of metal crunching against metal, the impact reverberating through the surrounding landscape. Shattered glass and twisted metal bore witness to the sheer devastation that had unfolded here. As a dedicated firefighter volunteer, I had always taken my duties seriously, but this moment served as a powerful wake-up call to the importance of what we were doing. In an instant, lives had been altered forever, and the once-pristine metal horses were reduced to mere wreckage.

Racing to the scene, we were met with a harrowing sight of three mangled vehicles, their occupants in dire need of immediate assistance. We quickly learned that, tragically, three precious lives had been cut short in a matter of moments, leaving three others clinging to the fragile threads of life. That heart-stopping moment, though it only lasted a split second, seemed to stretch on for eternity. The gravity of the situation left me grappling with an overwhelming sense of helplessness. I mean, I was only a kid; I wasn't equipped to deal with something like this! The desire to help others had always burned within me, but in the face of such devastation, I questioned if my efforts would even matter. Standing there, a mix of fear and uncertainty engulfed me—fear for myself, fear for those who had already lost their lives, and fear for those teetering on the edge of survival.

But amidst the chaos, as I stood frozen, a seasoned firefighter swiftly took charge, radioing for a medical helicopter without hesitation. Something within me immediately shifted; watching these brave responders spring into action, I realized I wasn't powerless at all—far from it, actually. It suddenly clicked that this was the reason I had trained for firefighting and the very reason why, I believe, God placed me on this earth—to serve and lend a helping hand. Though I felt small and insignificant, as we all do in moments of crisis, I knew that every helping hand, no matter how seemingly small, could make a meaningful difference. With that, the initial doubt and fear transformed into a resolute urgency, and I, along with dozens of other brave men and women on the scene, sprang into action. From that point on, the entire night seems to have gone by in a flash, owing to the adrenaline and fast actions. We were able to save the three lives, and I thank God for the opportunity and courage he gave me to ensure their survival. But the shock and sorrow lingered in the following weeks as I mourned those lost, haunted by the vivid memories of that fateful night.

Encountering the stark reality of life's fragility was an experience that left an indelible mark on me and the rest of the Second Brigade. From harrowing car wrecks to heart-wrenching medical calls, we bore witness to tragedies that most kids never have to face. But, in a weird way, I believe these experiences were crucial for me to fulfill my purpose. Witnessing such realities allowed me to grasp the gravity of my chosen path, to comprehend the true weight of the responsibilities I would shoulder. The phrase "life is short" is often thrown around a lot; life is short, so make the most of it; life is short, so hold the people you love close; life is short, so forgive and move on. But the true weight of this phrase hit us with full force when the consequences were so vividly evident before our eyes; life is so short and, in fact, so uncertain, that an everyday decision like overtaking someone could mean certain death. In that moment, we understood that life's brevity is not just a cliché; it's a harsh truth that can shatter lives in an instant. So, while it wasn't an easy path to tread, it was one I needed to walk to fully understand the seriousness of it all. This experience served as a poignant reminder that life is fragile, and in an instant, everything can change. Not only that, but it reinforced my commitment to serve others and cherish every moment, for life is indeed short, and our time here should be spent making a meaningful impact on those we encounter. It was a tough, eye-opening experience, but it taught me to value life's precious moments and appreciate the importance of quick thinking followed by swift action.

In the midst of it all, we formed an unbreakable brotherhood. Those late-night trainings and station hangouts were filled with laughter and bonding. Little did I know, those fast-acting decision-making skills we honed on the frontline would serve me well in my future business ventures too. Who knew firefighting could be such an effective business boot camp? Despite the challenges and heartaches, my journey in the fire department turned me into a more resilient, quick-thinking, and compassionate individual. It solidified my resolve to serve and made me believe that I could make a real difference.

Embracing the responsibility bestowed upon me by this new role, I juggled my church duties, my devotion to the fire department, and even my passion for baseball. Every Monday night, I dedicated myself to the fire department, attending trainings, meetings, and helping to clean and maintain the fire trucks. As if that wasn't enough, I also found time to work on a friend's farm, earning a few dollars to fuel my endeavors. I still fondly remember the long hours under the scorching sun, working tirelessly to gather hay bales on the farm. Though the pay was meager, it was more than enough to fuel my desire to serve and lend a helping hand whenever and wherever needed. At this point, my life was a grand slam of activities. Juggling church, firefighting, baseball, and farm duties made my schedule look like a wild rodeo—and I was the fearless cowboy trying to stay on that bucking bronco. Some folks might call it chaos, but I called it my version of fun.

Now, you might wonder how I managed to handle it all—trust me, even I sometimes questioned my own sanity. But like a finely-tuned baseball team, I had my secret weapon: quick thinking. When life threw those curveballs my way, I swung with all my might, adapting to whatever came my way. Maybe it was all a training ground for my future in business ownership, where I now wear multiple hats and dance between different roles.

This fusion of my involvement in the church, my dedication to the volunteer fire department, and my pursuit of various responsibilities painted a vivid tapestry of service that became an intrinsic part of who I am today.

However, I must admit, my academic pursuits were far from my strong suit. School, with its bookwork and math, just wasn't my cup of tea. While I enjoyed the fellowship, friends, and sports that came with it, the classroom setting left much to be desired. I was more of a hands-on learner, a low-B, high-C student at best, to be exact. Luckily, I found my solace in practical tasks and could easily work with my hands, fixing things, and learning as I went along. During summers, you'd find me helping my friends on their farms, tending to haybales, fixing tractors, or working with cattle—always eager to learn every aspect of the trade. As my junior year of high school approached, I knew I had to make a decision about my future. The dream of becoming a preacher and attending a four-year college seemed to be closing in on me. The thought of financial stress and endless classes deterred me from pursuing that path. I wanted to be outside and serve others in a different way, and that's when I began exploring vocational-technical classes, searching for the perfect fit to follow my heart's calling.

Chapter 3: A New Path Emerges

I belong to what Neil Howe and William Strauss defined in their generational theory as Millennials or Generation Y. No, I don't intend to start a debate about the behavioral differences between generations; that's for the experts. I made the reference to explain some of my youthful fantasies and how they were shaped by the changes taking place in that era. In the broader context, they also helped me become the best version of myself. Funny; read on!

I don't remember the 80s much, simply because I wasn't old enough. However, one thing that stood out for me was Back to the Future. It has Marty (Michael J. Fox) doing normal stuff like us, skateboarding and playing guitar, and not the usual cool heroic things. There wasn't anything fancy about him. He was the boy next door we all could relate to and imitate. Then there was Doc (Christopher Lloyd). Though I had inherited DIY genes from my father, Doc was the biggest motivation behind my love for machines. His inventive thinking, to create something new for the betterment of society, stimulated me. I know you must be thinking that it was a movie and everything was scripted, but the younger me, in the late 80s and early 90s, didn't view it that way. The movie pulled me like a magnet and prompted me to explore more in order to help others. For the young Brandon, exploring simply meant opening up any machine he could lay his hands on and then trying to put it back. Simple in scope but noble in meaning. After watching Back to the Future, especially Part II, my inner service provider was thrilled.

When I volunteered my services to presumably fill up the radiator of Dad's car, I envisioned myself as Doc Brown (Isn't it amazing we both share the surname; coincidence for others, divine for me.) with his lab coat on, working on his time machine. In front of me was not a Ford Taurus but a modified version of a DMC DeLorean with a huge flux capacitor, waiting to be fixed to embark on time travel. Unsurprisingly, my venture didn't go well, just like Doc's countless experiments. But just like him, such failures didn't deter me from offering my services. I still helped my friends with their barn chores, and the church staff to manage Sunday Mass and services. However, I must acknowledge that working with car engines fell below my priority list. The Back to the Future trilogy left an everlasting imprint on my life.

Another factor that played a big part in my internalization of the film was the dawn of the Information Age. The last two decades of the twentieth century saw great technological advancements impacting our everyday lives. Digital media started playing a bigger role as cable networks mushroomed. The internet also became a household name as the World Wide Web became public. Speedy access to information and ease of communication pulled down the barriers and painted a rosy picture for the future. With all these developments redefining our lifestyle, watching Marty flying on his hoverboard in Back to the Future II looked genuine; for once, the hype was real.

Social scientists define the 80s and 90s as the transitional period, and it certainly was. It was the time when cool gadgets started entering our lives. Admittedly, compared to the current lot, they appear as something belonging to the Stone Age, but when they first appeared boy, did they revolutionize the lifestyle or what. As a kid growing up in that era, we were the first generation to experience them firsthand. Yeah, you can say that we were the guinea pigs for the scientists and corporations to ascertain the feasibility of their products. But it is something I don't think any of us would complain about. Life was getting more fun, easier, and interesting, with a great scope of learning newer things in a relatively shorter period of time. Personally, my appetite for experimentation and *doing things on my own* was getting bigger and bigger. And I was loving it!

Therefore, when I approached the guidance department to discuss vo-tech options during my junior year and was informed about a new dual enrolment program that included HVAC, mechanical, electrical, nursing, cosmetology, and welding, I was excited. I was excited because here was an opportunity to learn technology from experts, keep myself abreast with what was happening in the world, and do something meaningful. More importantly, our county school was bearing all the charges. The program was free for the students, no extra expenses; they just had to work hard and learn. The two viable options were HVAC and electrical, with the scales more in favor of the former for some unknown reasons than the latter. Nursing, cosmetology, and welding were rejected even before the guidance representative finished naming them, and mechanical…well, I didn't want others to feel what my father did on that dreadful day going to the supermarket. I checked with the lady about the formalities and the paperwork required for the enrolment and left the office.

My high school was at that in-between distance from my home, far enough not to walk but not so distant by car/bike, so I usually used to drive the distance. My internal Mr. Scrooge had somehow reconciled to the fact that it wasn't worth saving the commuting money by walking to the school. In an economist's parlance, the opportunity cost was too high compared to the utility realized. Otherwise, I could be as miser as they come. Whatever money I used to earn as a part-timer was saved to manage my expenses like a responsible elder son. It was my way of giving back to my hardworking parents. Yes, I was into (occasional) partying and used to take my girlfriend on dates, but responsibility always came first.

Going back home, I deliberated on my choices. It was not an easy decision for me. One, by enrolling myself in the vo-tech program, I would be giving up on my preaching dreams.

Cool Success

It was a big call for me because I liked giving speeches in the church and attending other events. Being part of the church was akin to spreading the word of our Lord and was very satisfying. It was something I enjoyed doing on my own; our parents never enforced that on any of their children. Our family has always emphasized upon community work, so what better than being involved with a church? Religion and social work are both taken care of together. Therefore, whenever I looked at the enrolment form and thought about the vocational classes, a sense of guilt engulfed me. It was as if I was betraying God. For me, being associated with clergy was my internal calling. But I also knew my father needed his elder son to step up. Between the devil and the deep blue sea, religion and inner satisfaction or father! (Dramatical, yeah, but that's how we Millennials are.)

Second, although HVAC kept propping up in my mind, I was unsure about it. It was more of a case of *let's see what it offers*. And that was rather disturbing because I wanted to make a rational decision. My association with the church has inculcated a sense of ownership before deciding. Remember, haste is from the devil! I was raised not to take anything for granted, and honestly speaking, I couldn't afford it also. More importantly, my choice should be the one that can serve the community at large. It was all about we and not only me with me. Since I could remember, I have held this belief that if life gives you a chance to prosper, don't embark on that journey alone; instead, take others along. It was a product of my parents' upbringing, being part of a close-knit community, and church teaching. And I was not alone in upholding these ideals. Many of my peers ascribe to the same ideology. I, though, took it a notch above.

Therefore, I had, and still have, this habit of going through all the pros and cons of the available alternatives. My friends often used to make fun of me and ridiculed me for not *taking it easy*. But that was me, and I never intended to change. And here I was, having this strong urge, gut feeling, to select HVAC despite very little knowledge about the subject or the field. What should I do? *(Drum roles)* Let's discuss it with Dad and see what he advises. After all, as they say, there is no substitute for experience.

Back home, I shared the plan with my parents. They were supportive of my choice. Dad spoke highly about HVAC and how it would be greatly in demand in the coming years. I guess working at a store helped him foresee the scope of the field and its impact on people's lives; *no substitute for experience.* Their only concern was whether I would be able to manage all the load, which was very much justified. The dual-enrolment vo-tech program was designed in a manner that the first half, morning hours, was for the hands-on training at the community college, while the second half, afternoon hours, was for the studies at the high school. Commuting between the two required a minimum of fifteen minutes if one was lucky, so I wouldn't have much time to enjoy my lunch. Factor in my volunteer work at the fire department, and I would be all tied up for the day, even more than my father. They realized this the moment I told them about the course and were skeptical about its viability (they feared my burnout) but said yes just to make me feel better. My parents were proud of me for being responsible but worried about my well-being. I could see it in their eyes.

For ladies who think men are not good with nonverbals and don't understand your gestures and expressions, yes, we do. It is just that we tend to be selective about them; we call it priorities. I don't want to sound like a chauvinist, but think of it: the mood swings you guys have, it is impossible to cater to all of them. And it is always now for you guys. Even God is not demanding! Thus, as a part of our evolution, we men have learned to identify and rank the nonverbal signals. Then, it is all about satisfying them, one at a time, according to the situation and mood of the party involved. Reactions to the mother would be different from the sister and the partner. Priorities, knowing when and how to respond.

I know I owe an apology to my fellow men for spilling out our biggest secret, but I believe it was required to spare ladies from those anxious moments when they are unsure of our responses. The world is already tense enough.

The summer vacations were over, and I had to buckle up for long hours of rigor for the next two years. The only thing good about enrolling in the vo-tech program was that I was assured of my career path. In the 90s, with all the developments taking place, universities were constantly coming up with new degree programs and courses. For young aspiring minds without much guidance, it meant confusion and uncertainty. That's when I realized that sometimes having too many options could be detrimental as well; it can put you off from your target. No wonder I was the only student to have registered for the dual enrollment program. Another aspect, which I later realized, for my sole attendance was the glamorization of occupations. Everyone dreamed of landing high-paying jobs straight from college/university without getting their hands dirty. I don't know if it was the media or something else that created the mindset, but it was certainly prevalent. My philosophy was quite the opposite. I never loathed any occupation as long as it is teaching me something new, providing services to the masses, and improving their lives. Again, call it my humble upbringing or church teachings; that was me.

I had always been a keen, hard worker, not the one to trade work for rest. And if it was related to the church, all the better. If anything, my volunteer work over the years had made me a willing bull ready to plow any field any time of the day. However, with the dual enrollment program, I had to encounter a problem completely unknown to me. Often, I would wonder if I had bitten at more than I could chew. I was perplexed, even in a dilemma, because both classes were at the extreme opposite ends of the learning spectrum. While the vocational course, as the name suggests, was all about hands-on training, high school classes were the same, mundane theoretical stuff, something I had always detested. This tug of war, with no end in sight, was draining me. My heart was in HVAC classes, but, despite all the uneasiness, I couldn't do away with high school. I have to complete it for the certification. Being bad in maths, I couldn't equate RHS (right hand side) with LHS (left hand side) to balance the equation of my life. Well, certainly not for the junior year. My inequality expression always tilted in favor of the vocational classes both in terms of grades and fondness.

Being an eager learner, prepared for all sorts of work, I immediately took a liking for the vo-tech training. I can't recall missing a single class simply because they excited me. The challenge working with machines presented kept me engrossed; it was a riveting experience. However, not the same could be said about the regular classes. Theoretical stuff had always been my kryptonite and junior year was no exception. Concentrating during the lectures was the most tedious thing for me, and at times, I was caught dozing off by the teachers, which added to my misery. The junior year proved the long-held theory of every backbencher that teachers have favorites in classes, mainly the bookworms, and have little sympathy for others. *Hence proved!*

My problem was simple; I couldn't comprehend what we were learning without knowing its practical implementation. And since I was working hands-on in the morning, the urge had intensified. Everything coming out of the teachers' mouths used to bounce over my head, and I then had to ask my classmates for explanations. Private tutors were simply out of the equation. I guess that was the biggest drawback of our education system in our days—too much reliance on the bookish stuff. More than two decades have passed, and improvements have been made. Teachers emphasize more on self-learning from early years and allow their students to decide what to learn. A stark contrast from the 90s, when I was a student. This is not to undermine learning from books or theories proposed by great scientists and scholars. My point here is that academicians should devise an all-inclusive curriculum that can excite every student.

For a year, I merely flowed, scoring just the passing marks to keep myself afloat. As mentioned, at best, I was a low B or a high C type of student. However, during my junior year, I found it hard to even live up to my own (not very high) standards. And my grades took a beating. It was not as if I was not trying and shying away from hard work. No. It was just that the maze was too complex for me to find a way through. Whichever route I took had a dead end. Whatever I had tried failed.

But giving up was not the option available to me. My only motivation was that only senior year remained; one more year, and I would be out of the misery. I couldn't possibly go down at the last obstacle. Something needed to be done, but what? Work smarter may be.

With every ounce of motivation and dedication left in me, I dived into my senior year. Yes, you have read it correctly; I literally dived into it head-on. Cometh the hour, cometh the man. Well, the man had to come, otherwise, I would be doomed. And by the grace of God, he certainly came. My solution for the senior year was to go directly to God and ask him to enlighten the way forward. He knew my intentions were noble, and I wanted him to make up for my lacking so that I may cross this final hurdle. The more I imagined myself as the athlete lying on the floor just inches away from the final line on the 110-meter hurdle race, the more I shuddered. *Dear God, shower your blessings on your humble servant so that I may go on and help others. In Jesus' name, we pray. Amen.*

And like that, my prayers were answered. At the end of the academic year, I graduated from my community college and high school simultaneously, holding both certificates. Though I was happy and proud of my achievements, there was another man who was happier and prouder than me, Dad. His son has come of age.

Chapter 4: Embarking on a Career in HVAC

Before starting my professional life story, it is pertinent to share with you something that created a huge stir not only nationally but also internationally just before we entered the second millennium. (I started my first regular job around the same time in 1999.) The Y2K Bug or the Millennium Bug. For those who don't know what I am talking about, a little introduction. "A computer flaw, the so-called Millennium Bug, led to anxiety and the Y2K (Year 2000) scare. When complex computer programs were first written in the 1960s, engineers used a two-digit code for the year, leaving out the '19.' As the year 2000 approached, many believed that the systems would not interpret the '00' correctly, therefore causing a major glitch in the system"

Cool Success

https://education.nationalgeographic.org/resource/Y2K-bug/). For details, please check the provided link or Google the term Y2K Bug.

Now, in 2023, sitting in my living room, using all the advanced electronic gadgets, roughly thirty years after the news first broke out, I can afford to laugh it off. (As per my knowledge, the experts had started warning about the Y2K in the mid-90s, which created a huge commotion, forcing President Clinton to form a special council in 1998 to oversee the matters.) Then, it was a huge scare. The *IT experts* had all of us believe that once the clock would tick over to the next millennium (Jan 01, 2000), all the computers would switch back to 1900 instead of 2000 since they were only programmed to read the last two digits of a year. Therefore, systems would crash, destroying all the data stored. You have to understand that we are talking about 1999, and there weren't many external data storage devices apart from hard disks, CDs, and DVDs. Well, certainly not in general usage. Maybe exclusively for the government or the army.

It got the ball rolling. Literally, everyone panicked. Banks and financial institutions feared losing all their *precious* data, from customer information to interbank correspondence to lending and borrowing rates calculations. Imagine computers resetting to 1900 and changing the interest rate to what it was a century before; what mayhem it would have caused. Huge industrial units were fearful for their machinery. With all the systems going back, how would they reconfigure them to make their equipment work?

The most frightening news was that the defense department and army would lose control over the missile systems. There were rumors that the bug would launch the missiles on its own. Some media even reported such stray launches in Russia. Since the country was already in an economic and political quagmire, people believed that. (Later, it was debunked by the government.) Major developed countries even paid millions of dollars to IT companies and hired computer engineers to prevent any mishap.

Confusion abounded as all held their breath and waited for the impending doom. No one was sure as to what would happen. Fear of the unknown seeped through every individual. To further spice up the matter, the first movie of The Matrix trilogy was released in 1999. It showed how rogue technology overtook the world and enslaved its creator, man. Whether the writer, director, or the production team were inspired by the Y2K Bug theory, I don't know, but the timing was scary. Though in the film, our hero (Neo/Mr. Anderson) was able to fight against the AI team led by Agent Smith, not many were betting on this to happen in real life. *Will the IT experts be able to thwart the danger, or will it be as catastrophic as they are saying? Is this the apocalypse we have heard about before the Second Coming?* They all asked.

It is amazing, or rather infuriating, how, in the face of danger, people collectively return to God and religion. There were even talks of technology becoming redundant and mankind going back to the Medieval Era when everything was done manually. I believe it has to do with your internal response system, which craves for a messiah when up against an unsolvable problem. Then, Y2K certainly was one and needed a savior. As a species, we have the same fears and react similarly under the given circumstances. Then, why so many divisions? God created us as one and He wants us to behave that way. What went wrong? Something for the leaders, especially religious figures, to think about.

The fact that eventually, the Y2K Bug proved to be a farce and died down with a meek meow instead of a roar couldn't diminish the fear it had once struck in people's hearts.

***

I was out of high school and community college with dual certifications. If anyone had told me that I would be graduating from both educational institutions successfully simultaneously, I would have laughed, doubting the mental state of the person making such a prediction. Basically, I knew my scholastic capabilities. I was assured of securing good grades in my vocational course, but in high school…it was fifty-fifty, at best. What I, however, was confident of was my hard work. I did whatever I could have done and then left the matter to God. I just prayed to Him to help me and make things easier.

And He did!

Attending my high school graduation ceremony was a proud moment for my parents. I remember seeing Dad's eyes welled up. It was the first time I saw him teary-eyed. For me, he had always been the epitome of strength and courage. Come what may, and Dad would face it with a smile, without showing any sign of discomfort, remorse, or dejection. His I-got-it-covered expression is forever etched into my mind. I believe he knew how important his body language was for us, his family. He was our source of comfort, the shelter where we found refuge anytime, every time. And he would do anything to keep it that way by averting any sense of fear from coming our way. That's why he would never let up or lower his guard. Being the eldest son allowed me to share a special bond with him. He always made me comfortable to share anything under the sun with him. Plus, after observing my DIY aptitude, I was conferred the privilege of sharing his toolbox, something very dear to him.

Mom, well, we all know about mothers. The satisfaction I saw in her eyes that day was priceless and will forever remain my most precious and cherished achievement. By the grace of God, I have become a successful businessman, but no feat can beat that moment. Mom didn't say much because she was crying, and, honestly, she didn't need to. "Well done, my boy. I am so proud of you," was written all over her face. One of those magical instances where words are not needed to converse, as eyes do all the talking. If nirvana exists, it was there at that moment for me. I was in a land of bliss, the biblical

Garden of Eden, oblivious to my classmates and teachers. Nothing mattered more to me than watching my parents happy and satisfied. The moment didn't last long before everything returned to normalcy. However, it will remain with me till the day I die or even after. I can assure you that as I write this, I have goosebumps and a smile recalling all that over again. Memories!

To put the cherry on the top, I also landed a job. Double treat! Being the only person to enroll in the dual program helped me. It, in essence, worked like a recommendation letter for me. Many of my high school friends who went to college had to rely on their placement department for jobs, not me. My certification was my placement department. The fact that state authorities had initiated the vo-tech program got companies excited. Concord was not a big city, so tracing me was not a problem. And it didn't take long before my first job came calling. It was a local company, not a multi-national everyone dreams about. Then again, in my place, you will not find many local giants, let alone a multi-national. The company was basically based in Lynchburg and was catering to the customers in the adjoining areas from their city office. From

Concord, in those days, it was a half-hour drive, so traveling up and down wasn't much of a hassle for me. They specialized in installing and repairing HVAC systems in domestic and commercial buildings. Importantly, they were hiring high school students as apprentices, offering flexible job hours. There were other HVAC companies in Lynchburg, but they were not open to students. So, the company was a godsend. When I joined them, they had 40 employees. I was the forty-first, and the management wanted to expand; and enter Brandon Brown.

The fact that I actually passed the dual-enrolment program impressed my interviewer. It seemed he had analyzed that not only I was a hard worker but also someone who excelled in technical work. He didn't show much interest in my high school grades; my vo-tech certification was enough for him. Still, he asked some basic HVAC-related questions, which I answered correctly. After the interview, he extended his hand for a handshake and said, "I am sure you will hear from us soon, son."

And he was right. Within a week, I got a call from the company asking me to report to their office at the earliest with the relevant documents. Since I was free, no part-time, no volunteer work, and certainly no classes, I decided to turn up the next working day. *But, hey, I can't just walk into their office; I need to look professional. What to do?* I was excited but nervous. It was my first job, after all. I didn't want to be perceived as a novice unprepared for the rigors of the real world. Yes, I was a freshie, but I knew what it took to be a professional. Therefore, over the weekend, I went to Lowes and got myself some tools and a tool bag, something to impress my seniors. I was ready to leapfrog from being a student to an apprentice and onward to an HVAC technician.

It was Monday morning when I drove to my soon-to-be office. The company had a small parking lot reserved for its employees and visitors. I went in and parked my car. I looked at the rear-view mirror, hand-combed my hair, sprayed some deodorant to feel good, and climbed out. I walked to the main door in measured steps to avoid looking nervous. My heart was pounding at a rate of knots, but outside, I was like a calm sea; straight face, not even a wrinkle. *Just another day, nothing special!*

I went inside and informed the receptionist about the purpose of my visit. I submitted my documents and waited for the instructions. She called in to check for the relevant person in the services department (for which I was hired) to whom I could be directed. No success; all the line managers were busy in the customary weekly meeting as it was the start of the working week. Finally, she was able to connect with a lady who, though not directly a part of the department, was the only person on the seat. Availability trumped relevancy.

While the receptionist informed the lady about me and asked her permission to send me in, I looked around the reception area. It was not a huge office but well decorated, which showed the aesthetic sense of the company's management. I was impressed. They say the first impression is the last impression. Whoever had designed it sure knew what he (or she) was doing. The ambiance certainly got me hooked. I was overawed also because I didn't expect that from an engineering firm. You don't expect style or panache from them. Or do you?

"Mr. Brown, Ms. Emily will see you now."

"Ok."

"After the door, turn left and then second right. The second cabin on the right will be Ms. Emily's."

She passed me the instructions and got busy with her phone call. I thanked her, which I was sure she didn't hear, and went my way.

Inside the door was a completely different environment, typical of an engineering company, with huge posters on the wall showing the entire range of inventory and the projects the company had completed. I tried not to get distracted by all the artwork and quickly arrived at the destination.

Emily was a dispatcher, probably into her late thirties. She was the link between the sales and services departments. All the new orders were communicated to her, and then she used to schedule service teams' field visits. She would create a job card in the system, informing the services department about the client (name and location) and the services to be provided. For those who have worked in a warehouse or a manufacturing facility, a job card is somewhat equivalent to your delivery order. Though it may sound easy, liaising between two main departments, usually at odds with each other (we all know production and sales hardly reconcile), can be very taxing. The only way she could excel in her role was to be calm and organized and to always maintain a cooperative demeanor toward others.

And Emily was exactly that. Her sweet and assuring voice calmed whatever nerves I had walking to her cabin. She welcomed me into the company and offered coffee. Then she called in James, Benjamin, and Charles. They all were service technicians, with James being the senior most. Later, he also became our foreman. When they came in, she introduced me and explained the hierarchy. They were expecting another technician to join, which would complete their team of four technicians, including me, and a foreman. The team would then report to an engineer. I was hired as an apprentice and was assigned to James for training. There in started the most memorable phase of my professional life.

Being the senior technician, James was in charge of the service van. And he was very proud of that. He used to treat it as his most prized trophy. I know job attachment is a reality, and all (good) professionals like to take care of their official belongings, but with James, it was a totally different matter. His service van was the most well-maintained, always clean and ready for action. I can't recall an instant when he was missing a tool or running low on fuel. Everything was up to date. His discipline rubbed off on me as well. And eventually, when I got my service van, I used to look after it like James.

My orientation lasted for a couple of weeks. I was shown around the company and met all the relevant people. Being new to the field, I was also given some material to read. *Not again; I was here to work, not read!* The fun part started after that when I started visiting customer sites, initially with James and later with Benjamin and Charles.

I was finally introduced to the real world. Not a college classroom with a controlled environment and perfect settings. Then it dawned on me that when working in the HVAC field, one worked in all elements and weather conditions. I started my job near summer, so we were running service calls all day, in and out of the van into the hot sun. Temperatures were steady in the 90s with high humidity. Working in a service team, I got to know about tight attic and crawl spaces. Something I was definitely not prepared or trained for. It took me a few weeks to adjust and overcome my nerves and fears.

James, Benjamin, and Charles made learning easy for me, though. They were the best supervisors an apprentice could wish for. I never felt dumb asking questions, and they always offered me advice and help when needed. They made me feel comfortable from day one as if I was one of the guys. They inculcated a sense of belonging into me. I remember one day we went to one house; Benjamin had been there before but did not tell me. He said, "Ok, buddy, go in, do your thing, and I will come see if you're right in a few." I was thinking, *are you serious? Can I go troubleshoot on my own?*

I jumped out of the van, grabbed my bag, and went to the front door. I entered the gate of the fenced-in front yard with excitement to tackle my first call. I knocked on the door. As it opened, two dogs came toward me, looking to attack. I turned and took off, running to the gate. I finally got out of the gate and looked into the van with Benjamin laughing so hard he had tears coming out of his eyes. He stepped out and said, "I am sorry I forgot about those dogs. You need these treats and they will love you." After realizing I had been set up for Benjamin's pleasure of watching me run from dogs, I finally laughed it off; he knew the whole time I would be chased out of the yard.

I took to the work like a duck to water. Even my seniors were surprised. As per them, they hadn't seen any young apprentice so eager and willing to work. The nature of our job included getting one's hands dirty and working in an uncomfortable environment, hot and often humid. Not what an entry-level technician has in mind when starting. But I was there for a cause, to provide my services for the betterment of society. Hence, I couldn't afford to sit idle and waste my time. My exuberance proved contagious and played a defining role in experienced technicians' acceptance of me as one of their own. They started teaching me all the tricks of the trade, which increased my productivity exponentially, even forcing the management to take note.

Therefore, at the young age of twenty, the company promoted me to the position of lead service technician and gave me a service van. Think of it; I had a service van at my disposal. Not bad, Gordon! But I knew it was just the beginning. Now was the time to be more attentive to the work in hand. I had to show that I was worthy of their trust and my performances were not a fluke or dependent on my seniors. Yes, they taught me and were responsible for whatever I knew about HVAC systems, but my hard work and dedication also played a major role in grasping whatever they had to offer.

Cool Success

I had to show to my management that not only was I a good technician but also a good leader in making, who could look after the company's assets, either machinery or human resources, well. Earlier, I had seniors to fall back on; honestly, they covered up many of my mistakes. You can say it was part of my learning curve; one couldn't learn without making mistakes. However, all three were very cooperative and considerate. They saw the urge for greatness in me and poured everything they knew into me.

I remained with the company till 2005 and can safely say that whatever I know about HVAC is down to those three gentlemen. They took me under their wings and trained me like seniors should. They were so thorough with their training that after a year under their tutelage, I knew everything about the system, like the back of my hand. I knew about all the faults and how to fix them. I consider myself lucky to have them as my guide; I couldn't thank God enough. It is certainly His grace that made this possible.

Chapter 5: Answering the Call to Serve

Everything, good or bad, comes to an end. That's the beauty of life; it is always moving ahead, springing up surprises along the way. Sometimes, those surprises give us instant gratification, like getting a promotion or a new job. Others, though, are not so favorable and force us out of our comfort zone. Social scientists usually refer to them as the highs and lows of an individual's life. Whatever the case may be, both highs and lows are there for a reason: to align our paths with God's. Often, during our lifetime, we become too individualistic or self-centric and lose sight of God's plans. We forget that we all have a divine purpose to fulfill: to serve humanity to get nearer to Him. That's when He throws up those surprises. They act as stumbling blocks, allowing us some time to sit back and think about our thoughts, priorities, lifestyle, goals, and direction. Basically everything.

Cool Success

I don't agree with the notion that only when a person is down and out for the count does he realign himself with God and track back. For me, it's a myth! Yes, people generally become 'more religious' during difficult times, but I have seen people returning to their Lord when He has showered them with all His blessings. They consider themselves unworthy of the favors the Almighty is conferring them with, and hence, try to return the favor by giving out from whatever they are receiving from their Lord to people in need. Those who only remember Him when in distress can be called seasonal worshipers. (I know this term is also used for those who only worship on holidays, but I hope you are getting the point I am trying to make.) As soon as the wind changes its direction and they sense the dawn of a new spring, their course changes.

***

My stay at the company was nearing its culmination; I could just sense it. Like a hunch one develops over a period of time and not some knee-jerk reaction. I somehow was not getting the same satisfaction from my work as I used to. Something was amiss.

Economically, the dawn of the new millennium couldn't have come at a better time. The US economy, which started its recovery in the '80s and made significant progress in the '90s, progressed forward in the first decade of the twenty-first century at full throttle. It was way ahead of other countries, justifying the tag of the sole superpower. Our great country was in a league of its own, not just militarily but also economically. All the indicators were positive, forecasting great days ahead. The real estate sector benefited the most as financial institutions lowered their home loan conditions. Result: a majority of the people owned property on a mortgage.

Our field of work, HVAC, is associated with real estate. Therefore, the upsurge in property demand translated into an increase in HVAC sales. As numerous buildings spawned on every nick and corner of the country, our workload escalated. And with that came monetary benefits. I moved up the ladder in the organizational hierarchy. Considering that I was still young and single, living with my parents, and without major responsibilities, you can say I was going through the purple patch of my life. Good earnings, but not much of expenses. However, my inner self was not satisfied. Was I ungrateful or unappreciative of what God has given to me? No. Instead, it was on the contrary. All these materialistic gains left me feeling that I was leading a mechanical life, something which I had never desired. My dream of being a good and responsible citizen was getting neglected. I wanted to be one but couldn't identify the avenue to translate my ambitions into actions. I was experiencing the greatest dichotomy of life: despite having a stable and rewarding job, I wasn't feeling happy. I wasn't myself. *Is this what it means to get stuck in the vicious circle of a materialistic world?* The more I try to escape to find some solace, the greater the world's lure and charm. My life seemed like a maze with no exit!

Then I stopped trying. When in doubt, leave it to God to lighten the way forward. I just flowed with the tide and waited for His guidance to get me back to the right path. I wasn't doing anything wrong to be ashamed of, but I wasn't doing anything right as well. Getting up in the morning, going to the office, returning in the evening, having dinner with family, and sleeping was my whole routine. There was no meaning, no purpose in what I was doing. The reason why I joined the HVAC, to serve the community, was lost somewhere in the economic activities. *When nothing seems to be going right and you can't find the way, trust in God to lead you away.* My soul's call was answered, though, in the most unusual of ways.

In 2005, Hurricane Katrina battered the southeastern and southern coasts of the US. The devastation was so massive that the Federal Emergency Management Agency (FEMA) launched a nationwide campaign asking for volunteers to work in the devasted areas for rehabilitation. As I heard about it, I knew this was the moment I had been waiting for. It instantly clicked and I signed up. But my chances were very slim. The destruction caused by the hurricane had united the nation, much like the dreaded 9/11. Hundreds and thousands of people from across the country offered themselves and signed up. Therefore, getting selected from a remote area like Concord was nearly impossible. I didn't care about that and did what I had to do. And voila, one fine morning, I got a message from the agency asking me to confirm my availability. Initially, I couldn't believe my eyes. I had to double-check to assure myself that it was true. FEMA has selected me and another gentleman from Concord. The agency's communique informed us that our services would be required for a 30-day campaign and we would be sent to flood-hit areas along southeastern and southern coasts. Additionally, we would be paid on an hourly basis, but that was inconsequential. I was not volunteering to earn. I was volunteering to serve.

I immediately called my line manager and informed him about the situation. I told him that I had to go; there were no two ways about it. Unwillingly, but knowing I wouldn't change my decision, he allowed me to go. He said, "I will hold this job for you for 30 days in case you change your mind and come back. Take care of yourself." I was grateful to him for being concerned but knew changing my mind was not even an option.

My partner and I packed our bags and headed out for Atlanta, where FEMA had set up their base camp. Once there, we were given basic first-aid training for a couple of weeks and later were sent to Florida. Florida was the first to take the hit by Hurricane Katrina and was in immediate need of support. We were stationed in the southern region of the state. The horrific scenes I saw there are hard to describe. Don't think I have seen anything worse, and I have seen much. For someone who had watched Miami Vice in his younger days, the image of Florida was of warm weather and exotic beaches. A perfect holiday spot for us in the north. Watching its areas submerged in seawater was so frightful. Imagine the sea, which had been the emblem of calmness and relaxation and a source of income for many, getting rowdy and destroying everything in its path. I had seen the images of wreckage on national media before coming, and those footages were disturbing, but watching it live was beyond comprehension. Everywhere we went, buildings were torn down; hardly any remained unaffected. Some had injured people trapped inside, some had dead bodies. And this was after the initial batches of volunteers had already worked on those areas. Imagine what they must have witnessed! I used to shudder at those thoughts. No wonder to date, Hurricane Katrina is the costliest and deadliest hurricane to have ever hit the US shores. The enormity of the relief work required made it beyond the scope of FEMA. Hence, global institutions like the Red Cross joined in and set up a temporary shelter to accommodate the affected. Similarly, friendly nations sent their troops to assist with the cleanup and rebuilding. It was like we had entered a warzone. Well, it was a war, not against any belligerent nation or an extremist group but against nature. God save America!

I was in a team of six, two each from Concord and Oklahoma and one each from New York and Oregon. All my teammates were very highly dedicated and motivated. They all had left their jobs and comfortable lifestyles just to help their fellow Americans in their time of need. We had banished 'negative' thoughts like how would my family survive without me, and would I be able to rejoin my office on return? At that moment, it was all about the nation for us; personal comfort was out of our priority list. Very much like our brothers in uniform.

We were assigned multiple tasks, primarily related to evacuation and transportation. All the heavy work, digging, clearing, excavating, etc., was carried out either by the army or the concerned authorities. Since I had firefighting experience, it was a bonus. I tried to impart whatever knowledge I had of handling traumatic situations to my teammates. And they all used to listen and follow me. It was amazing because they were much older than me. I was the youngest by a comfortable margin; all of them were above thirty while I was in my early twenties. Still no egos. We were there on an important mission and were prepared to learn whatever was possible from each other without any prejudice or bias.

Three weeks passed by in a jiffy. Every day, we would travel to different locations, carry out FEMA-assigned tasks, and return late in the evening to our rooms. That was our bonding time. For an hour or two after dinner, we would sit together and share personal stories. It was a great learning experience for me. It helped me learn more about life and appreciate whatever blessings our Lord has bestowed upon me. Blessings that I usually took for granted but which were luxuries for some. Every night before going to sleep, I used to say my prayers, thanking God for whatever he had given to me. Those pep talks also taught me much about problem-solving and team-building skills. I got to know that a problem could have multiple solutions. All we had to do was choose the most feasible option and act according to the situation at hand. Therefore, one must always be open to learning and accepting different points of view. They allow an individual to assess the situation well and arrive at a better solution. A wonderful lesson for a person with a progressing career in front.

Cool Success

On the 25th day of our work with FEMA, the agency gave us two options: continue working for another month or return. I had been dreading leaving the place because I badly wanted to stay. There was so much more to do. I knew going back would hurt me more with the extra baggage of that unfulfilled feeling for life. *What if I had stayed longer?* Therefore, FEMA's message was a blessing; I was staying. However, my partner left. I think being around a devastated area and regularly meeting with people who had literally lost everything took its toll on his mental health. He looked disturbed in his last days of stay. Though he was trying his best, one could see that he was fighting a lost battle. Looking back, I think he made the right decision. Had he stayed, it would have proven more cumbersome to him and maybe his family. Let's not forget he had already given a month of his life to the nation. Away from his loved ones and without much comfort.

I had another problem, though. Staying for at least another month would mean being away from my job. I had promised my boss that I would be back as soon as possible. For him, that meant thirty days. And now I have to ask for another thirty-day leave. Oh, brother! *A man has to do what a man has to do.*

I somehow managed to call him and inform him about the latest development. I knew he would be angry, but I didn't want to keep him in the dark through false promises. We had mutual respect for each other, and I wanted to keep it that way, irrespective of my employment with the company. Unsurprisingly, he wasn't amused. He was shocked that I had decided to stay for another month without any regard for my job and family. He didn't know that I was home and the people I was working with, and for, were then my family. Nothing else was required. Again, knowing that I wouldn't budge, he didn't say much. Honestly, there wasn't much to say. Disapprovingly, he accepted my decision. However, he had a word of caution for me. "Brandon, I respect what you are doing. But now I can't guarantee that I will be able to hold the job for you. I hope you will understand."

I knew that was coming, so I just said ok and hung up.

Though Hurricane Katrina made landfall in Florida, it gathered speed when it entered the Gulf of Mexico and caused even more devastation there. New Orleans, Louisiana, was the most affected city. That was not all. Mississippi, Alabama, and Georgia got hit as well.

Cool Success

As the epicenter of the hurricane, and consequently, devastations, shifted, so did the locations of our relief work. We moved around Arkansas, Louisiana, and Tennessee, trying to rehabilitate the people all along. It was not easy but was necessary, like the house chores, which had to be done whether one liked them or not. There was no way out. So, we stayed our course. Soon, the second month neared ending. Again, we were offered the same choices, and again, I chose FEMA. In this way, the one month that I had offered my services for turned into three months. I just couldn't find the courage to leave. My countrymen were in need; I had to help them. The biggest motivation behind serving for FEMA was that it was the answer to my prayers. I was the one who had asked God to give me an opportunity to serve Him. And now that He has provided me with one, I just couldn't turn my back on it. End of debate!

The only downside was that I lost my job. Though it proved to be a blessing in disguise, more on that in the next chapter, it did hurt me a little then. It was my first company. I had learned all about my work there, had made friends, and met great people. There was a lot to cherish about the association I had with the company. Therefore, I didn't want to end it like that. The day I received the voice message informing me that I was no longer an employee of the company was a tough one. Now, as an experienced professional and as an employer, I can decipher the logic behind their decision; back then, it was a bit hard pill to swallow.

Despite being engaged in the relief efforts, FEMA allowed us a week's leave and arranged for our travel back home for Thanksgiving. It was highly appreciated for more than one reason, as that one week proved to be life-changing. While back home, one day, I was hanging out with my friends when one of them, Elizabeth, introduced me to her friend Dara. I had heard about her, but it was our first meeting. And that altered my life. Within moments, I knew she was the one I would like to spend my life with. I enquired with Elizabeth about Dara and came to know that she had just parted ways with her boyfriend. An opening for me! But I have to be cautious. Elizabeth warned me that Dara was not interested in any sort of relationship. *Oh, boy, I have to earn my love. As they say, there is no free lunch.*

Cool Success

Before I could formulate a strategy, the week was over, and I had to report back. Nevertheless, I managed to get Dara's number. I decided to keep in constant touch, more in a desperate attempt to climb up her friendship list from just friends to good friends and maybe more. Another volunteer work. But this time, it was for myself, as my life was at stake. Conversely, I had much to gain as well. So, I had to be careful and opportunist at the same time. Soon, we were on talking terms. I used to call her every night and talk with her for hours. Patience is a virtue, and thankfully, I was self-sufficient in that. One step at a time, I built our relationship, ever vigilant not to be hasty. A wrong step, and she would be gone. With so much in line, I just couldn't afford a mistake.

By the time my third term neared its end, Katrina relief efforts were winding down. Thus, FEMA offered me to either move to the western part of the country to help with wildfire efforts or return. For once, I chose to return. My heart yearned for Dara. I wanted to meet her and know more about her. My FEMA life was over, but it gave way to the most beautiful phase of my entire life. Me spending time with Dara!

Chapter 6: Starting a Business and Overcoming Challenges

In numerous church sessions, I had heard that having an appreciative partner is God's blessing. Our Creator has created us in pairs; if man and woman understand each other and are willing to go the extra mile, life becomes that much easier. I was not alien to such a relationship. I can proudly say that Mom and Dad still are one of the best couples I have seen in my life. They truly were made for each other. The level of understanding between them was something to admire; it inspired us also. Most of the time, just a glance was enough for either of them to know how the other was feeling or was trying to say. No words required. In fact, relying on words to act as a messenger would have been a waste of effort, an insult to their love. Just a look and message conveyed. Being their children, sometimes we were clueless as to what the two were up to.

Cool Success

Growing up in an era when the divorce rate peaked in the US, we were lucky to have both parents together. It also used to make me think, what made them tick. How come they were so comfortable with each other? Yes, there were disagreements, even quarrels, but they were exceptions. And wouldn't prolong. Even as children, we knew *normal services* would resume sooner rather than later. I asked Dad about this often. He would only reply, "Once you will find the love of your life, you will know. The significance of keeping her happy will dawn upon you because if you won't do it, your life will be a mess. You will feel restless. Then, you will make all the sacrifices willingly. The same will apply to the partner; it takes two to tango!"

Sound advice. But initially, these words couldn't satisfy me. On the contrary, they seemed a bit far-fetched. How can two different people connect so well? Were Mom and Dad behaving like that simply because they have gotten used to each other? And upsetting one would force the other to come out of their comfort zone? That was why they were happy to maintain the status quo; the proverbial *don't rock the boat!*

I used to have such stupid questions whenever I thought about my parents. Pretty dumb, I know. Though I never expressed them in front of anyone, the One who knows everything, knew about them. Then He decided to show me the other side: *What it is like to be in a relationship.* That was when Dara came into my life. And at what an appropriate occasion: Thanksgiving!

Christmas was approaching when FEMA allowed us to return since Katrina relief work had all but winded down. I was super thrilled because I would be able to spend more time with Dara. The mere notion of being with her, talking to her in person, and (maybe later on) holding her used to get me excited. Honestly speaking, till now, I had never been in a serious relationship. Church and volunteer work, and later job, had kept me busy. So, it was new for me as well. And something I was anxiously looking forward to upon my return. When our relationship developed into something substantial, I started to realize the worth of Dad's words. *"The significance of keeping her happy will dawn upon you because if you won't do it, your life will be a mess. You will feel restless."* Truer words have never been said. Nothing could summarize my feelings for Dara better than these words. Though I had never admitted it in person before, I started feeling prouder of my parents, especially Dad. He seemed to know everything, and had a solution for every problem. Experience, love, parenthood; whatever it was, it was magical. Like a fortune teller, he could predict the future.

However, that was not all. I was returning home jobless! FEMA had compensated for our services well, but what now? An uncertain future awaited me.

With not much in hand, I started searching for jobs. But it seemed nature had other plans. Dara knew how quickly I grew as an HVAC technician. She was adamant that I should start my own business. She still hasn't revealed what made her believe that I would be able to manage a company; I am not complaining.

Upon her insistence, I looked out for opportunities and found out that a guy was selling an HVAC work van full of stock, parts, tools, etc., for $2,500. Pretty cheap! The problem was I didn't have the amount. Ruefully, I shared the information with Dara. There was an opportunity for me, waiting, but I didn't have the money to afford it. The agony of being so close yet so far was overwhelming. I almost broke down in tears. Dara listened carefully to what I had to say, tried to console me, and, after some time, left. While leaving, she asked me to keep believing and everything would work out. I thought she was just trying to make me feel good. No! She went home and discussed with her dad to lend out $2,500 to me. *"The same will apply to the partner; it takes two to tango!"* Dad, you are an oracle.

It meant the world to me. Not just because I had the money to buy the service van but because there was a girl who believed in me, in my dreams, more than myself. And was prepared to go to any length to help me and make me happy. You can't imagine how rejuvenating that feeling was for me. Suddenly, I felt like having the world under my feet.

I had no idea how she convinced her dad. I never bothered to ask because asking her would be akin to disrespecting her feelings. I only knew one thing: come what may, she had my back. It motivated me no end. The hard worker in me found the vision to move ahead. In January 2006, we launched Brown's Heating and Air.

Having said that, nothing came easily to us. There already exist several companies that have experience and a strong customer base. They held all the cards, but we were not to be discouraged. The turn of events made me believe that everything was happening according to God's plan. My part was to work hard, honestly and sincerely. Rest the Planner would take care.

As expected, the first year was tough, not just physically but emotionally as well. Finding customers was very hard and I had to rely on my reputation to win service contracts. However, what was even harder was the degrading behavior of the seniors. People whom I have worked with for years turned against me and made fun of me. They ridiculed me for *turning against them*. They treated me like a traitor and waited for my defeat. Hoping that I would come back to them, begging for an opportunity. I was having none of it. If anything, their behavior made me even more resolute. I banished any thoughts of winding up my company and working as an employee for a stable income. *I have a reputation to defend and defend it, I will!*

Thanks to the economic boom, Brown's Heating and Air made enough money to see through the first year. The second year brought with it new opportunities and contracts. While founding the company, our philosophy was simple: respect your customers. 'We are a customer-centric company' was our motto, and we genuinely believed in it. We went out of our way to customize our services to provide maximum satisfaction. And soon, results follow. Orders started pouring in and I found it hard to manage everything alone. Therefore, I hired a part-time guy to help me with services and maintenance work and subbed out the duct-related jobs. It helped me concentrate better.

2007 gave way to 2008, and halfway into the year, the slide happened. Now known as the worst economic recession in a century, it all started as what was called a market correction. Economists termed it as a logical outcome of the overheating of the economy and predicted a quick return. But it never came. An economic downturn turned into a recession, which nearly turned into a depression. Businesses went down like dominos, especially financial institutions and real estate. Century-old companies filed for bankruptcy and went out of business. The government intervened, but by that time, the damage had been done.

Cool Success

Like others, Brown's Heating and Air also dwindled. My payments got stuck, which hampered my cash dealings. One builder who owed me $25,000 suddenly went out of the radar, leaving me clueless as to how to pay my vendors. Research shows that the majority of businesses close within the first three years of their operations. Our company was in danger of being one of them. I feared becoming just another statistic to prove the study correct. I wanted to be a part of the minority, which survived through the initial years and lasted for ages. But how to achieve that was the biggest question mark. Air has taken out of our business due to non-payment. Vendors were constantly calling me, but I couldn't do anything.

What to do? How to get out of this quagmire? Potential investors were not interested in making any significant investments, fearing any loss. Banks were already chasing for their outstanding, let alone lending more. I wanted something to happen and I wanted it to happen quickly. Time was running out.

Out of desperation, I contacted my local bank, with whom I had been working for some time. I talked to the manager, explained to him the situation, and asked if the bank could loan me $25,000. Surprisingly, he agreed. I said surprisingly because despite having a good working relationship with the bank, I wasn't expecting it to come to my rescue. *Never lose hope because help can come from any quarter.*

The day the amount was credited into my account, I started repaying my vendors. It helped build the image of the company. The movers and shakers of the industry started noticing us as potentially a future star. *If a company is paying its vendors in such a financially weak situation, it must be maintaining a good balance sheet.*

After starting and managing my own company, I quickly realized that my nescience of sales management and financial management was hurting us. As a technician, I had good knowledge of the operations side but was not well-versed in others. And it was the Great Recession, which forced me to correct my course. *Every cloud has a silver lining!*

All our initial contracts were down to my reputation as a technician. As I had said, I belonged to a small community and people tend to know everyone around. Similarly, builders and developers of the locality knew me as an upcoming HVAC serviceman who had come through the ranks in a relatively short span of time. I was a part of one of the reputable companies in the area for more than 5 years, and almost all the contractors knew me. I had worked on their construction sites, either installing a new system or servicing an installed one, and had developed a good working relationship with them. This healthy PR helped us secure early orders. I tried to utilize the positive word of mouth to my advantage, and it paid dividends as well. However, there was a limit to that. I lacked the nuance of proper sales communication to hook new clients. In sales parlance, that's called a *sales pitch*, which I realized I had to learn. It was not that I didn't know *what to say*, I simply didn't know *how to say it*. That's the art salespersons have; they know what their clients want to hear and word their message accordingly. This helps them get the attention of their audience. As an operations person, I had far more knowledge of an HVAC system, but usually, a salesperson would get the deal simply because of their speaking power. It was one of the most important lessons for me: *one doesn't have to say everything; say what the other party desires to listen*. In the corporate world, no one has the time and patience to listen to your stories. They just want to know whether you can satisfy their needs and deliver on your promise. If you somehow manage to convince your client, the deal is yours. All the new sales professionals out there, this is my advice to you. Learn about the buyer you are dealing with and deliver your message, sales pitch, in such a way that it resonates with him and persuades him to think that you are the best solution provider. In this day and age, your buyer is not interested in fancy jargon; he is only interested in whether you can satisfy his needs. If the answer is yes, you are in. Otherwise, you will fail to make a mark, no matter the brand you are selling.

The other area I suffered in was financial management. Being from a nonaccounting background, I used to believe that it was not different from maths. Add the revenues and minus the expenses, and you have the answer. I mean, it couldn't be more complex than this. Boy, was I in for a reality check or not!

First of all, sorting out the expenses was a headache. The problem was not that I was not making money; the issue was that I was not being able to hold on to that. I was simply not able to recognize the reason for the *leakage*. When I worked on that, I got to know that I was not alone. Those who are not well-versed in accounting, like I was, find it difficult to allocate expenses to a given project. For example, if I was working on 5 projects simultaneously, then what I used to do was accumulate all the expenses under one head. Therefore, upon getting payments, I would start making payments irrespective of the fact whether that amount was spent on that project. This wreaked havoc with my financial matters. Though I was in the good books of my vendors, I was always left wondering *where did my money go?* In such a scenario, if a client fails to pay on time, which happened during the 2008-2009 recession, I was the one facing the financial crunch.

Here, it is very important to clarify that by above, I don't mean to encourage holding vendors' payments. No. I am only saying classify which expense was incurred under which project and then make out payments. This way, you will be able to know how much money you made on that, and secondly, you will be in a better position to reinvest it back into the business. As you are reading these lines, these things will look simple to you, and you may say, "Oh, this is common sense." However, in reality, these are not that simple. Maybe because common sense is not that common. Being a sole entrepreneur looking after all the matters alone, such things often slip out of your mind. You find them too trivial and concentrate too much on getting sales and providing the best customer service. It is of utmost importance to keep track of your expenses. No wonder those accountants make so much money. They deserve it!

For me, though, I didn't have to look to anyone to come to my rescue. Dara was my messiah, again. She was in college at UVA . She first helped me with getting the bookkeeping right. I had only heard about financial statements like profit and loss statements and balance sheets; it was she who taught me how they were made. Her biggest contribution, I believe, was to start project-based accounting. Dara told me to start treating every project as a separate entity, hence, maintaining different account heads for each of them. Jumbling up all the expenses would serve me no purpose apart from being in my vendors' good books.

Looking back, I believe those circumstances went a long way in strengthening our relationship. I was an operations guy and found communicating with clients far easier. I worked on sales management and improved my communication skills but needed a trusted person who could watch my back in terms of financials and give me sound advice. And Dara did it. We complemented each other really well. We defined our areas of responsibility and stuck to them.

It also, kind of, furthers my belief in God's plan. I was sure that He had sent Dara into my life for a purpose. And that was to help me build a business that can serve the community. That difficult period also instilled a desire to learn more about business management. I didn't want to surrender meekly. But in order to survive through troubled times, I needed to know more. I was prepared to go to any lengths to make our business work, not just for me or Dara but for the community and those attached to the business.

Chapter 7: Embracing New Opportunities

The greatest beauty of life is the uncertainties it throws at you as an individual. At first, they may be unsettling and discomforting, forcing a person to come out of their comfort zone; in the long run, they are beneficial. I can hear your groans. But seriously, thought about it rationally. Those who are going through a tough phase, I pray that you come out of it quicker and better. However, at the same time, I will ask you to reflect back on how you were before. You must have seen those 'Then and Now' challenges on social media. Take some time and analyze yourself without any bias. I am sure you will come up with more positives, and it will cause a smile to spread on your face. Go ahead and allow yourself a satisfying and wholesome moment.

If you are wondering why I am so confident in making such a bold call. It is simply because that's how nature works. One of the most important lessons I have learned in my entire life is that nature has a set pattern and works according to it. If you break any rule, it will throw your life off track; you may call it course correction. However, it will present you with ample opportunities to come back on track and lead a prosperous life, provided you are willing to change and adhere to those laws. Another instance when a person endures a tough period is when they are about to receive something big but are not ready for that. Again, the laws of nature will throw them off to let them acquire the requisite skillset so that they can handle and manage the next big assignment better.

However, and it is a big however, the above conditions will apply if a person is honest and sincere in getting out of the rough patch in the first place. Let me put it bluntly: whining about unfavorable conditions will not help you make your way out of them. On the contrary, it will only elongate the duration. The difference between successful people and average people is this mindset only. A person who only cries about lack of opportunities will not get opportunities. And the reason is they are not doing enough to create opportunities for themselves.

There are approx. 8 billion people in this world and the majority have access to food. (We are not talking about drought-hit countries here.) The issue is in the difficulty level with which they can acquire it and the resources available to them. Those living in developed countries can't complain about that. We should be thankful that we are leading a luxurious life in comparison to others despite our constraints. Then, what is the solution?

As a person, it is in your hands whether you decide to put in the hard yards initially to reap the benefits later on or not. Hard work at young age provides a person with a head start over others, who take matters casually. That's the rule that has been constant throughout the annals of humanity, and I don't see it changing anytime soon. I firmly believe that a person makes his own luck. I have seen people inheriting billions and losing them because of their indiscipline. However, it doesn't mean the late boomers can't make it big. They can, but for that, they have to do away with their unproductive habits.

So, guys who feel the rub of the green is not going their way, go ahead and do an analysis. Think hard about yourself, your attitude, and your lifestyle before the downslide and now.

Cool Success

If you see a positive change, congratulate yourself and get yourself a drink; you deserve it. But don't stop; keep moving forward because only then will you reach the desired destination. And if you don't observe any internal transformation, then rest assured that you are not sincere enough to get yourself out of that hole. You are not willing to come out of your comfort zone and consequently have created a catchy slogan 'lack of opportunities' to hide behind. This scapegoating attitude will not get you anywhere. The saying 'there is no free lunch' is true. Therefore, go out, work on yourself, and alter your priorities. Get your hands dirty, and I promise sooner rather than later, you will be reaping the rewards. Let me tell you, there is no better feeling than enjoying one's own success.

What's the idea behind sharing all this with you? After all, it is supposed to be an autobiography and not a self-help book. Answer: because that's what I did after the Great Recession. Whatever I have mentioned above is the hard-earned wisdom of those difficult and strenuous days.

In the previous chapter, I mentioned how we launched Brown's Heating and Air. We because Dara has been very much part of the company since the start. In fact, without her, I wouldn't have been an entrepreneur.

Till the financial crunch of 2008, I had a very smooth ride. Yes, I had to balance between the vocational course and my high school classes before, but that was my own decision and I was happy with that. Apart from that, my life had been on autopilot. Soon, after completing my course, I got a job where I met great people and learned a lot. And when Hurricane Katrina came, I left to work for FEMA. Later on, I met the love of my life. Then, I started my own company, which found success. All in all, it can be said that my life was following a perfect script till 2008-2009. I had lived the way I wanted to, without much stress.

That was when life threw me a curveball. I know the Great Recession was hard on everyone, but it was harder for me because I hadn't faced such unhelpful conditions before. My business had been running for 3 years, and just when I thought of finally settling down, everything crashed. I went into debt and had to borrow money from a bank to pay off all my dues. Basically, it was like taking a loan to get rid of the debts. The only positive was that there was now only one creditor.

Cool Success

The downturn forced me to start searching for a job. I wanted to marry Dara and start the new phase of my life. But without a constant, fixed income, it was not possible. The bigger problem was that following the real estate market, the HVAC industry also nosedived. Though I applied to multiple companies, there weren't any suitable vacancies. The majority had closed down, and those who had survived were in no mood to hire. What to do?

At that time, the local fire department was hiring. I took the opportunity gleefully. Remember, I talked about coming out of the comfort zone to move ahead; for me, that was it. I had given a good 7 to 8 years to HVAC. All my professional learning and experience was in the same field. However, at that time, it couldn't guarantee me a stable income. Had I not availed the opportunity, I would have missed a great prospect to rebuild my business and career. Hence, I dropped the idea of finding a job in HVAC and switched to firefighting. It helped me greatly to get back on my feet. Firstly, it assured me of a salary. Secondly, and more importantly, since I was working 24-hour shifts, it allowed me to keep track of my company part-time. The flexibility permitted me to relaunch my company better.

Brown's Heating and Air was Dara and mine first child, and I was in no mood to let go of it easily. During the initial phases of the recession, I realized that I needed to upgrade my skillset to equip myself better in business management. Thus, I enrolled in communication and financial courses. The idea was to upgrade myself so that I could analyze the situation top-down. As an experienced employee, I had a good idea of tactical matters: how to manage operations and keep the clients happy. However, I lacked strategizing. And, hence, my decision-making suffered. To overcome the deficiency, I needed to improve myself. I knew nature had great plans for me, but I was not ready to shoulder the burden. Maybe that was why I was thrown off to learn and get back on track.

Being from an operational background, I didn't have much knowledge about financial matters. Honestly, I hadn't thought about it also. My mindset was similar to new entrepreneurs entering the market: take care of the operations and keep your customers happy, and the business will take care of itself. To a certain degree, I was right, but one can't just overlook financials; that's akin to leaving your bases empty, which is not a very good strategy for the long run. Yes, it is good to be customer-centric but know your limits. After all, accounting people are the ones who give the top management the true picture regarding the cash flow. They know when the company has enough *in the tank* to go for an aggressive sales approach. My experience now tells me that sustainability should define a company's way ahead. Often, we get too excited with new orders coming in. However, we should always keep an eye on our current situation and question ourselves, "Is it feasible?"

Life is about balancing our options to arrive at the optimum solution. Economics 101: humans have unlimited wants and desires but limited resources to satisfy them. Thus, it is imperative to let go of lesser utility options. Read it on the first day of my economics class, but it stuck in my mind. I still remember it! And why not, in my opinion, it should be one of the basic rules of our lives. Everyone should know about it and follow it, not just the economists. It is easier said than done, though. New business owners get too excited with sales orders and go overboard to complete them. In the process, they forget about the cost they are incurring. That's why most businesses shut down within the first three years of their operation; they run out of steam. Reason: their owners had over-committed without keeping their cash flows in mind.

Sales and marketing guys will never get tired of advertising or promotional campaigns. Ask any of them, and they will say an organization should actively engage with its customers. But whether it is feasible at a given period of time is to be decided by the management, and that's where accounting knowledge comes in handy. That's where you require qualified accountants. They are the number crunchers of the enterprise. After getting stuck in the precarious situation of having to pay off $25,000 to my vendors without a penny in the account, I realized the importance of having a grip on financial matters and learned about preparing and analyzing financial statements. Talk about having to learn the hard way!

And learned I did. I was working as a fireman, providing HVAC services, and learning business all at the same time. It was one busy schedule. However, my past experience came in handy. I was used to hopping around multiple places, and this was just an extension of that. But with one exception. Unlike before, I had a clear goal in my mind. While earlier, it was more about social work and giving back to society, this time, it was all about making big as a businessman. I was willing to go the extra mile. The fact that I wanted to get settled with Dara further motivated me. I barely got to meet my friends, but I never complained. I was looking at the bigger picture and it was showing light at the end of the tunnel. It gave me hope and filled me with motivation to keep moving ahead. Looking back, I now realize that had I stopped in my tracks then it would have spelled doom for me. I would have stayed there, as a firefighter and wouldn't have been able to fulfill my dream of owning a company that gives back to society. I am by no means degrading the firefighting profession. I am just stating that I wanted more out of my life. I wanted to make an impact at the societal level. And for that, I needed to put in that extra bit of effort. I did and can safely say that I am now reaping the rewards.

April 30th, 2011, was when Dara and I exchanged vows. I can't recall another instant when I was that excited as when the preacher proclaimed us husband and wife. It was one of the moments, if not the moment, of my life. In this regard, I'm old school and believe in having a proper family. Temporary relationships are not my cup of tea. I'm not belittling anyone; just expressing my ideas, so please don't judge me!

My parents, siblings, and friends were there to wish me luck. Our marriage function was held in a local church. Standing near the altar alongside the father, I was having butterflies in my stomach. Strange, really, because I had known Dara for a good 4-5 years; she had helped me set up the company and was constantly looking after the accounts. From the first day I saw her, I knew she would be one, and when it was happening, I was feeling anxious. Was it the setting or the reality dawning upon me that I would be a family man? For some, being in the spotlights, I was the groom, remember, can also throw things off. God knows. Dara's entrance into the hall in her pearl-white dress calmed my nerves. She looked at me and smiled. It was the most beautiful smile and reassured me that everything would be okay. No matter what, she had my back. 13 years have passed, and it is still the case.

Once our honeymoon period was over, I got back to my hectic schedule: a firefighting job, business projects, and studies. Dara had known about my engagements; hence, she got along easily despite me not giving her enough time. I felt bad but was in no position to let go of any of them. The job at the fire department was necessary for a smooth income stream; providing HVAC services was also important for me to remain an active player in the industry; and courses were the need of the hour to upgrade my skillset for smoother and better management of my business.

There are moments when a man feels tied down and helpless, but that's when the Creator is weaving His most beautiful tapestry. As His humble servants, when encountered with such situations, we only have to trust his judgment and keep moving forward. I know, at times, it can be difficult, but that's the test, the challenge. Don't let your fears get the better of you and follow His path. A man is most vulnerable when he is either financially or emotionally down. That's when the doubts creep in and he starts questioning the logic behind his Lord's judgments. Little does he know that God is always planning good for him, and it is the impatience on man's part that throws everything off.

In 2011, we welcomed our first son, Parker. I still remember holding him for the first time. There was a surge of excitement, happiness, joy, and elation. Reliving those moments still gives me goosebumps as if it had happened yesterday. His arrival presented me with a new challenge. I wanted to spend more time with my young family to share some of Dara's workload; I wanted to be with them as an assurance that I was around in case they needed me, but I couldn't. I had to wait. For Brandon, the husband and father, it was very agonizing to spend more time away from loved ones. My rational mind tried to pacify the matters by suggesting that whatever I was doing was for them. But that logic was not enough. For once, I felt dismayed. That's when our gracious Lord showed me the way to calm my nerves. As our creator, He knows our limits and helps when it is required the most. It motivated me to keep going in confidence that He was watching over us.

I, on my part, tried to remain steadfast as much as possible, and soon, our Lord showered his blessings on us. It was 2015 when our business finally started to flourish, so much so that I gave up my firefighting job to concentrate on the business. I landed on mega projects that predicted a constant, stable income for the foreseeable future. I needed extra hands to complete the work in time, and therefore, I hired 4 employees on a permanent basis. They were the first full-time employees of our company. That was the second coming of Brown's Heating and Air. And since then, we haven't looked back. Interestingly, that was also the year when our second son, Dawson, was born. For many, it can be a coincidence, not for me. All along, He had been planning this and it was the perfect time to reveal it. Why? Because I was ready to take on the mantle. As I had said earlier, sometimes life throws you off the track because you are not competent enough to handle the responsibility. That was what happened to me. Had God given me the success earlier, I would have wasted it. Instead, in the beginning, He gave just enough to make me realize my shortcomings. It was like Him telling me, "You deserve much more, but you are not ready for that. First, go and prepare yourself to be able to accept and hold on to my blessings." And once I was ready, He didn't hold back.

Chapter 8: Scaling Up and Learning to Lead

Growing up, I was more into baseball than any other sport. During our spare time from school and church, all the neighborhood friends used to gather and play ball. As mentioned earlier, I belong to a small town, Concord, near Lynchburg. Though it is an old town dating back to the eighteenth century, designed mainly as a train stop, it never developed much. Part of the reason was that the railway moved to Roanoke, which grew manifold consequently. Therefore, Concord remained a sparsely populated farming town. While it made for excellent countryside viewing and a laid-back lifestyle, something everyone desires nowadays, the downside was that we didn't have enough players to play baseball.

As a young boy, one of my main struggles was to get enough kids together to form 2 teams. Age didn't matter as long as they were willing to join us. Yeah, the struggle was for real. Almost every time, we ended up playing homerun derbies, which, though not desirable, couldn't be avoided. *Something is better than nothing!* It was only when our friends or cousins visited us from either Lynchburg or adjoining areas that we got to play a ball game. Even then, it would be 6 or 7 players on either side, and the match consisted of 5-innings-a-side. But it was great fun. Getting to play your favorite game imitating your favorite player was every boy's dream, and I was no exception. The player I looked forward to the most was Chipper Jones of the Atlanta Braves. I was so obsessed with him that I used to keep track of all his stats, like batting average, hits, home runs, and RBIs. I still remember in the 1999 season, he won the National League MVP award. It was like a personal achievement for me, and I threw a party to my friends. In those days, for me, Chipper was baseball, and baseball was Chipper. Yeah, those were the days; typical fan adulation!

Usually, our lucky days, when we had ball games, fell during summer vacation. Every match has that sense of fulfillment as if we had achieved something substantial. Being able to play was an accomplishment in itself. Our passion and verve used to drive us forward, which I must admit paid me rich dividends later on. My association with the church and scout organization has made me a natural leader. But I was very much a rough diamond who was polished by sports. Wondering how? Let's continue.

We had found an open field to satisfy our thirst for the game. However, it was not in the best of shape. Together with the elders, I arranged a complete overhaul of the place. On one side was a tree line, so we made it our boundary, the home run line, and designed the playing area accordingly. Admittedly, it was not the best ballpark one could ask for, but at least there was something to enjoy our beautiful game. The quest to find a solution instead of whining about the problem was inculcated in those early days. Hence, I unknowingly developed a problem-solving approach. Similarly, I was the one to gather all the neighborhood kids and set out to play. It strengthened my leadership skills, and I got in the habit of *getting the job done*. The small jigsaw pieces were coming into place, completing the beautiful picture our Lord had designed for me. Looking back, I sometimes wonder how I managed to perform all those tasks. Nowadays, even completing one job makes me feel exhausted. Youth, maybe. But I believe it was the Will of God. He wanted me to experience that tough routine because He was preparing me for something extraordinary.

My passion for the game led me to the high school baseball team. For me, it was akin to graduating from neighborhood team to high school team, at Rustburg High School. Luckily, our school did have a playing field of its own, which was a relief. Our coaches had divided our practice into 2 sessions: the first one was workouts. For that, we used the school gym; that was what we liked to call it. The second was ground practice, which meant pitching, hitting, and catching. And fortnightly, we used to have a role play, where our coaches would form 2 teams and let us play against each other. Team practice used to take place after school hours, which during summers was taxing, but our passion knew no bounds.

My high school baseball career sadly didn't last long, mainly due to my volunteer service at the fire department. However, I was a regular in our neighborhood matches. Moreover, Rustburg used to host Little League matches. Being near to my house allowed me to take part in the competition. My spring used to be very tough, attending school and then traveling to Rustburg for matches. But it was fun and something I never complained about. In hindsight, I believe such a hectic schedule caused me to become a tough nut.

My athletic body, with great reflexes, lent itself naturally to being an agile fielder. Though my idol was a third baseman, I usually used to field at either first base or outfield. If my memory serves me correctly, that was the first and most significant decision I took for myself. Earlier, it was always what elders thought best for me. Hence, I acquired another skill: decision-making. Little did I know that those baseball matches with my friends, for mere fun, would go on to make a significant impact on my life. I learned team-building and a never-say-die approach, developed patience to accept different points of view, and polished whatever leadership skills I had. More importantly, I started trusting myself. Talk about building self-respect and self-esteem. Nothing better than doing it on the ground in front of others to see. No wonder researchers and academics stress so much on extra-curricular activities. Looking back, I realize how important they are for young and developing minds.

Moreover, coming from a close-knit but small community like Concord helped me to internalize diversity very early in my life. After entering the corporate world, when I started traveling to different places, I realized and observed that people in general, had issues interacting with those from different backgrounds. Maybe because of prejudice or bias; I didn't know because it was new to me. For me, or should I say all the Concordians, no such problem ever existed. Basically, there were so few people that we couldn't afford to discriminate among ourselves. The small size of our community has made us more welcoming, irrespective of others' race, religion, and political ideas.

The most I had to rely on those sports-inculcated skills was during the pandemic. As the financial crunch subsided by 2016, industrial activities made a comeback. Confident with the measures adopted by the then government, investors poured money into the market, and soon, everyone was envisioning a boom similar to the lines of the 90s. I was also witnessing growth on personal and professional levels. Personally, Dara and I had welcomed our sons. And professionally, I was able to win major HVAC contracts to relaunch Brown's Heating and Air. It was my second coming as an entrepreneur. The Great Recession had tested me to the core. Physically, I had to work on multiple fronts and study as well. I was overworked and drained, but I couldn't complain. There was no alternate!

The stagnation was equally taxing emotionally. I longed to spend quality time with my young family. I sometimes felt desperate to be with them, to hold my sons, and help out Dara. However, it was not to be. As our baseball coach used to say after a bad game, "It wasn't your game, boy, chin up. No need to feel bad. It wasn't your fault; you have to realize that your opponents are also there to play and win. Sometimes, you triumph over them, and there will be times when they will get the better of you. The result doesn't matter; the most important thing is to fight till the end and never throw in the towel." Never throw in the towel practice helped me during those difficult times. After realizing that I was not alone and everyone was equally affected, I brazed myself for the long haul. My gut feelings told me that the situation wouldn't return to normal for some time. I was prepared for the match to go into extra innings. So, as a defensive infielder, I needed to be alert; I couldn't afford to let my guard down. Focus, Brandon, focus. And when it was my turn to bat, try to connect as best as possible.

And I did exactly that. I knew not only mine but the lives of my young family depended on me. I wasn't alone. I was a family man and had to act accordingly. With an unflinching faith in God, I kept swinging hard, hoping for a letup. And it came. The markets rebounded from the slump, and soon, the opportunities followed.

However, the worst was yet to come. Just when everyone breathed a sigh of relief that the worst economic conditions in a century were over, the pandemic happened. Everything came to a standstill, literally. I had never envisioned a scenario where meeting people, the loved ones, would be banned. But it happened. Being an outgoing guy who liked meeting people and interacting with them, it was infuriating for me to stay indoors. I have to admit; at times, I used to question the government's policies of imposing the Lockdown. Instead of fighting the disease, they were forcing us to keep ourselves locked as if the virus wouldn't enter our houses. Having said that, I never doubted their intentions. It was just that we were passing through extraordinary times, which demanded tactful decision-making, not popular.

During the first month of 2020, when President Trump announced a public health emergency due to an outbreak, I was like, "What the Heck! Not again? We just got back to breathing properly."

Just when I was getting the grips of the strategic aspects of a business, we went indoors. The last 4 years were smoother than I was expecting. Orders came in, staff grew, and so did the revenue. Top of the chart was the service and installation order for a 250-apartment complex that I had won in 2015. The contract expired in 2018, but by that time, I was strong enough, financially, to leave my day-time fire department job and concentrate solely on Brown's Heating and Air. The order propelled my business, forcing me to hire more employees and increase the service van inventory. The sweet fruit of patience and hard work. I came to realize what God had planned for me and the route I needed to take. It was so comforting, not just the success but also knowing that you are on the right path. The one your Lord has chosen for you. The next step: keep going and don't slip up. Don't let your new-found success get to your head and blind you from the teaching of God. The One who has been masterminding your success and guiding you through all the ups and downs. Again, focus, Brandon, focus! The match is not over yet. Yes, we have hit a home run and taken a lead, but it will not take much for the Devil to even the score. Don't let him crawl his way back. Now that you have Satan pinned, keep him there.

From the past experience, I learned my lesson and became ever more vigilant. *Once is a mistake, twice is a stupidity*; these old sayings carry weight. Despite the short-lived business boom, I had already made a provision to place shock absorbers to soak up any untoward situation should it arise. I wasn't wrong in my assessment because it didn't take nature long to turn the tables. I was back in the ballpark with our lives at stake. Will I survive another grueling innings? Or will it be too much for me? Only time will tell.

The pandemic changed our world in more ways than one. Work ethics and norms took a 180-degree turn. On-site job conditions became less stringent, making way for work from home. Even when on-site presence was mandatory, businesses ensured the minimum possible attendance. The fear of meeting an unexpected end forced people to open up, not just in their personal lives but also professionally. Why? Because the world had woken up to the reality of life: death.

I have this hunch that the advancements man has made in the medical field are due to one reason: delay death. Ideally, man doesn't want to die and wants to stay in this materialistic world. There are many reasons to that; one is the fear of the unknown. Since no one knows what will happen on the *other side*, people view death with skepticism. As if it is taking away something very precious from us. The notion has made us as a whole terrified. We don't want to die! But is it the right approach?

According to the Scripture, death is nothing but going to another world where everyone will be rewarded according to their deeds. Hence, those who follow the Word of God in their lives will have nothing to be afraid of. They will receive their due reward from their Creator. What a contrast. On the one hand, we have fear and hopelessness, while on the other hand, we are told to celebrate death because that's when a believer will see his Lord and enter His paradise.

COVID-19 brought all these topics, which had been pushed back, to the forefront. It put a mirror in front of the humans to see their true faces. And it terrified them. Terrified by their own deeds, which they had buried, hoping not to confront them again, ever! But that's not how nature works. It always finds a way to come back and haunt man by showing him his own face. Karma. If anything, COVID-19 showcased our frailty in the bigger scheme of things. It was something we were unwilling to accept. It displayed man's weakness and forced him to search for the true source of power, the Ultimate Being.

For businesses, the pandemic was a double-edged sword. Yes, it caused problems, forcing many companies to shut down. Yes, it increased unemployment due to the Lockdown. But there is another aspect to it. COVID-19 also opened new avenues. I know many individuals who made substantial money through freelancing and offering online services. As a business owner, I believe the pandemic was a trendsetter and provided new opportunities to humanity. It afforded us another perspective of doing business. I know many of you must be questioning my ideas, to put it mildly, but think over it rationally. Just like every coin has two sides, every problem has an inherent opportunity. This is a universal truth that can't be rejected. The catch here was whether we, as a whole, managed to identify that opportunity. The answer to that question, I am afraid, is no. We paid too much attention to the turmoil and forgot to analyze the situation judiciously. To be more blunt, I believe that instead of coming out of our comfort zone, we stayed put. And to justify the loss, we all made COVID-19 the scapegoat.

Like other companies, Brown's Heating and Air initially took the hit. Fear gripped our employees, who were reluctant to work at sites, and customers, who stopped issuing orders. Nobody was sure what would happen. Everyone was scared of the unknown. However, soon, our staff got the hang of things. Together we all realized that something needed to change. We just couldn't wait for things to move in our favor. Someone has to take the bull by its horns. I raised my hand, hoping God would see me through. And He did. He made our employees stand firm through the difficult period, fully conforming to management's decisions. Collectively, we worked out a method to keep our business rolling while being safe from the virus. Innovative methods were proposed and adopted to satisfy our customers' demands by providing the best of our services. As an entrepreneur, I firmly believe that the pandemic gave us the best opportunity to work together as a team for one goal. Something that was missing before because of excessive working protocols. COVID-19 brought them down, bringing management and staff to one point. It did wonders for Brown's Heating and Air, and I am sure many organizations benefited as well.

Chapter 9: Reflections on the Journey

Recollecting my memories while writing this book in Nov 2023 makes me realize how lucky I am to come out trumps after experiencing everything life has to throw at me. I am 42 now, and in those years, my eyes have witnessed some great moments of complete joy and ecstasy, moments when a person feels like a ruler of the world, along with those of nerve-wrenching sorrow, when you are down and out waiting desperately for the referee to complete the count down and stop the match, but the beating continues. And I am not the odd one out. As they say, if you live long enough, you will get to see the ups and downs. So why do I consider myself lucky? If everyone goes through the same process, why do I believe I am privileged? How am I different?

Before replying to the above queries, let me be clear: I am not claiming to be better than others, nor am I saying that I am

Mr. Perfect, who has decoded the mysteries of life. No, there is absolutely nothing like that.

If I were to pinpoint the biggest achievement of my life, it has to be my connection with God. That has been the essence of my stay on this beautiful planet, which has only grown stronger with time. At times, like any other curious individual, I couldn't comprehend the setbacks I experienced. Despite doing my part with all honesty and hard work, I faced failures. This left me emotionally weak and vulnerable to abandon the path and go astray. It was very hard to hang on, and had it not been for my parents' strong Christian teachings, I would not have been able to reach where I am today.

One of the basic principles Mom and Dad taught me was that our mental prowess is not enough to understand God's plan. Therefore, instead of using our faulty logic to make sense of the proceedings, we should leave everything to the Best of the Planners. He created us and knows what is best for each one of us. He has plans for every individual and we should stick to it. It is our transgressions that bring us undesirable results, but we don't realize them; some even go overboard and blame Him. I mean, how unreasonable and ungrateful a man can be!

Later, while studying business, I understood the meaning behind the principle. During an economics class, our professor told us about ceteris paribus. Literary, the term means holding other factors constant. In economics, it means while studying the effect of one variable on another, the effects of other variables are held constant. The professor went on to say something that clarified some of the earlier mysteries which had troubled me. At a given time, multiple variables impact a given variable, and it is not humanly possible to ascertain the exact effect of every one of them. That was when it clicked. We are simply not capable enough. No wonder the Scripture teaches us not to delve into all the matters. We are only told to do our part, i.e., work diligently and honestly and leave the results to God. Why? Because we don't know which forces or variables are in play. Thank you, Mom and Dad, for teaching me the ultimate principle. I don't know whether they knew the logic behind it, nor do I care, but I know it saved my life multiple times. Whenever in doubt, do your best and leave the rest to God. Life can't be simpler.

I have observed that normally people spend more time thinking about the outcome than doing something to achieve that outcome. We worry more about something that is not in our hands. And that is the reason why the majority went astray. There is no point wasting your time on fixing an uncontrollable variable. Instead, try to fix the controllable variable, like actually doing it. This will give you more satisfaction, and even if the results don't go your way, at least, you will gain some valuable experience. I know many of you might be thinking, but what's wrong with planning? Nothing; instead, planning is essential. However, one must understand that only planning about things will not bear fruits. A person has to act as well. And when executing a plan, don't think about the outcome. Don't jump the gun or try to get ahead. I know it is difficult, but it is very important: try to stay in the present and the future will take care of itself. Having said that, I am all for continuously reviewing the plan. It keeps a person updated about the progress and the direction in which the project is heading.

Another field in which I applied the same rule is business. After founding Brown's Heating and Air, I quickly realized that I was not good at keeping records. I knew my forte was technical knowledge and customer service, and I relied mainly on that. For the accounts, I just counted on Dara to come good.

Dara…now, this is one mystery I am still unable to resolve. I was busy volunteering for FEMA, trying to provide relief to the survivors of Hurricane Katrina. I was so committed that not in my wildest dreams was I thinking about returning home, let alone entering into a relationship. I had already extended my stay twice, resulting in serving for 90 days from the original 30 days. Then, the organization sent us home to take a breather. Constantly traveling to devastated areas and meeting with affected people had a negative impact on many of the relief workers. Back home, I was out with my friend, Elizabeth, who introduced me to her friend, Dara. First meeting, and I knew she was the lady of my dreams. Upon my return to FEMA, I never felt the same. Thankfully, their relief operations were winding down, and I returned permanently. Talk about the perfect romantic movie script straight out of Hollywood.

Innumerable random events take place in our lives, but not many leave an everlasting effect. Meeting Dara was one, which again made me go over our economics professor's words: *it is not humanly possible to ascertain the exact effect of every variable.* But for the Creator, nothing is impossible. He knew that FEMA operations were coming to an end and also that I had lost my job. Hence, He brought Dara into my life just at the right moment to start phase 2, entrepreneurship. In His master plan, the time has arrived. Eighteen years have passed, and for me, this is still incomprehensible. All the puzzle pieces fell into place on their own, and bingo! Before I knew it, I had a girlfriend who became my wife and a trusted business partner. The relationship has lasted some of the toughest times and is 18 years strong.

The other day, I was attending a local community seminar as a guest speaker. At the end of the session, there was a Q&A session where the young students and professionals asked me about my recipe for success. I said, have faith in God and trust your instincts. Do what you are good at; remember, don't just think or plan, act also. These two lines are the summary of my 42 years of life. I learned it the hard way, though.

The second biggest learning of my life is having no expectations or keeping them at the bare minimum. Cumulatively, we are habitually taking everything for granted.

We assume that life will continue on its tracks smoothly, without any hiccups. Hardly will you find anyone talking about making provisions for hardships in their life. Why? Everything that goes up will have to come down. That's the basic rule of this world. Still, the majority skip it and never make it a part of their planning. Many don't understand that, unlike other creatures, man has the power to make decisions. Those decisions, whether right or wrong, impact our lives with far-reaching consequences and alter our path. The resulting change defines the new us. Now, it is up to us how quickly we accept that change and act accordingly.

Assuming specific scenarios repeating themselves for infinity prepares our minds for certain outcomes. As if our lives are similar to the sun rising from the east and setting in the west, following a predestined path day in and day out. We don't consider a twist along the way taking place. That's when expectations grow. We expect people to remain and behave the same all the time. That doesn't happen in real life. People and situations change, and we, as mature people, need to accept that and move on. Failure to do so lands many in awkward situations. In my personal observation, that was where the pandemic hit people the most. It forced them to change their lifestyle and perspective toward life. Initially, individuals and societies resisted and only changed after the realization that there was no other choice. The time it took to realize a change was required and actually act upon it defined the level of loss societies and countries experienced during the pandemic.

Again, this is the truth I learned the hard way.

As if COVID-19-enforced changes to our business and personal life were not enough, we ran into some family health issues. Once, I went in for a normal physical check-up. There were no problems, and the trip was more of what we technicians called a preventive measure exercise. However, the doctor dropped a bombshell, saying that he observed a mass near my throat. He instructed me to get some tests done to ascertain what it was all about. The revelation threw me off. Here, I was going in for a routine check-up, and instead, the physician told me that I might be having cancer. I wish no one has to go through what I endured then; the relentless panic and scariness of those next few weeks were overwhelming at times. I underwent several tests, with doctors initially telling me it was cancer and that I needed to act fast. Oh Lord, what the hell is going on?

After multiple scans and biopsies, I finally got the call: "it is benign but needs to be taken out." Well, that was a relief. I didn't have cancer. Still, I had to get surgery and was referred to UVA in Charlottesville. It happened during COVID-19, and I had to go through all this alone. Dara was not allowed to accompany me. For me, that was the scariest part: experiencing everything alone. Then, I further realized the importance of a partner. No wonder God has created in pairs. There is a logic behind that.

That was not all. At the same time, we also had Dara's gran at home in hospice, who passed away right after my surgery. One of her uncles, Carl, was diagnosed with lung and brain cancer with not much time of life expected.

How can all this hit at once, and how will we get through this? Those several months were very hard on all of us and our families. Losing Dara's gran and her uncle soon after my scare really put a different vision of life into our heads. We learned to be grateful for whatever blessings our Lord has showered on us, not taking anything for granted.

Cool Success

I consider every moment spent with family and friends as a blessing. Cherish your loved ones and the time you do have. Maybe the COVID-19 lockdown, looking back, was not so bad in the long run. It gave us more time at home together.

Conclusion: From Success to Significance

Life—the most beautiful yet most complex phenomenon. You will attend hundreds of lectures, watch multiple videos, and will read numerous books on the topic, still none will be able to define it in totality. At max, those speakers and writers will only present their versions of life and how they understood its reality. Nothing more than that. And you will not find anyone claiming that, not even the best of the thinkers. It is not that nobody had thought about it. Many delved to explore the true meaning, and will continue to do so, yet all of them remained clueless. They couldn't comprehend the mystery it presented despite looking so simple. So simple that everyone takes it for granted, and so bewildering that no one has been able to come up with a befitting definition. Why? Because life is enormous with uncountable facets. Humanity is still in the process of discovering them, let alone mastering and explaining them all.

Working closely with people from all strata of society over the years has provided me an opportunity to witness firsthand some of the most fascinating thrillers. Analyzing them, one marveled as to how every piece of the puzzle fitted in perfectly and completed it in the nick of time. Very much like a script out of Hollywood, or even better than that. I can surely say that even the most avid thriller lovers will verify that reel-life mysteries are no match for their real-life counterparts. Because human minds write cinematic scripts, but real-life drama is the work of some supernatural being. There is someone up there who is continuously updating our life stories. Mind you, I am not dogmatic. So please don't go ahead of me. I believe in free will, but I also believe that a super being is working parallelly, and his plans are so strong that they can supersede ours. I prefer to call that super being God.

I am not a philosopher, but I do possess a curious mind. And like every inquisitive soul, I have tried to study life from my own angle. The aim was first to understand it and then choose a path to reach personal goals. I have always believed that goal-setting is a product of one's perception of life, like what they think of life and intend to take out of it. In simple terms, you can say it is the purpose of life. In business terminology, we call it vision. Fulfilling that purpose brings satisfaction and happiness. Since everyone has a different perspective, their cause or source of happiness is also not the same. Hence, social scientists have failed to identify one definite source that makes a person happy. The most they will say is that if a person is doing what he loves and performs well, he will be happy. Beyond that are different theories, up for debate and close examination. Happiness is very subjective and differs from person to person.

Our outlook defines our attitude, interests, and priorities. Coming from a close-knit community with strong religious values, I perceive life strictly from what has been ordained in the Scripture. From as far back as I can remember, our parents have always inculcated a 'we' culture in all of us. There was no 'I' in their dictionary, and the same was passed on to us. We were encouraged to think about others, which included society and not just family. It was their way of serving the Lord, who had informed us in His book that looking after fellow human beings is akin to serving Him. Therefore, it was only natural for me, the eldest son, to indulge in social work and church activities. You have read all that in the earlier chapters and I don't want to repeat them here. However, I want to mention the purpose behind those activities. Please read on.

Lately, we have seen how mental health issues have crept up and become a burning issue. Not so long ago, a person discussing anxiety or stress was looked down upon. It was considered a taboo and nobody wanted to talk about it. Popular opinion was that man shouldn't be sharing such information as it didn't coincide with his tough image. Silence, however, didn't eliminate the problem. In fact, it multiplied and now professional therapists are encouraging everyone to discuss their emotional condition often. Why, as a species, have we reached this point? Isn't this the era of opulence? The technological advancements and, consequently, financial upgradation should translate to more satisfaction and mental stability. Why is it that an individual is more depressed despite having access to all these luxuries?

The answer to all these burning questions, according to me, is due to individualism. Over the years, in the quest for success and physical gains, we have marooned ourselves. Everyone is looking for their own benefits, often at the cost of others. And once that target is achieved, a person feels empty and inconsequential, with nothing else to do. It is then we experience insignificance, something our brilliant mind can't accept, and a person goes down the wrong way.

So what's the cure? In my opinion, realigning with God is the only viable option available. Think about it. He is the creator of everything. He knows us inside out, better than ourselves. And appropriately has laid down commandments in His book for our benefit. So that we don't go astray and experience mental meltdowns. He knows us, that's why He has created the cure for all the diseases. We only had to follow the lead.

Following the Scripture by word also makes a person more social. He understands the suffering and tries to play his part. Remember, it is not about completely wiping out the misery. No, the God doesn't want that. He wants every one of us to play our part. Do whatever is possible and then leave the result to Him.

Cool Success

I am so grateful to our Lord, who provided me with the resources to play my part for the betterment of humanity. All that was asked of me was to remain honest and steadfast. The two most essential traits of any successful individual: honesty and steadfastness. The former keeps a person focused on the final target, the goal that needs to be achieved. It diverts all the distractions that may hamper the progress and derail all the effort. But it doesn't come easily. It demands high levels of concentration, passion for the cause, and belief. Only if a person possesses all three does he manage to remain honest. Else, the world, with all its charm and beauty, will allure them and dump them into oblivion.

Steadfastness is using willpower not just to overcome internal demons but to fight against all the odds in the physical world—the disappointments, the failures, the rejection—and keep walking on the chosen path. I believe steadfastness is very much a logical extension of honesty. Only an honest and truly loyal person can remain steadfast to their cause come what may.

I can safely say that I ticked both the boxes. Coming from a humble background, I had to work very hard to be able to realize my dream of providing relief to my people in whatever sense possible. At times, I felt like swimming against the tide, going against societal norms like when I volunteered for FEMA despite having a job. But I know that was the right thing to do then. I knew my calling and responded.

God has never said that His path will be easy to walk on; if anyone lives in that delusional world then they should look at the sacrifice of Jesus. Despite being the Son of God, He had to suffer so much, without any fault of His own. When an individual decides to follow the right path, they should brace themselves for difficulties and challenges. However, one thing is for sure, victory will be theirs, provided they remain honest and steadfast.

I don't claim to be a saint. I just did my part and in return my gracious Lord has rewarded me with aplenty. First, He gave me such a loving family. Secondly, He made me a respectful and prominent figure in the society, as proof of which I will share the list of the individual awards at the end. Lastly, and more importantly, He chose me for His work.

I had never dreamt of being a writer. However, after seeing all the negativity in the world, I decided to share my story with you. I don't want any validation of my success from anyone. The objective behind writing this book is to tell you that if a small boy from Concord could do this, so can you. I was very much a boy next door that everyone can relate to. Born without any golden spoon in my mouth, I climbed up the ladder of success by the grace of our Lord and my commitment to His path. And that's how I want to end my book with— trust yourself, but more importantly, trust the One who created you. He knows what you are capable of, just stay patient and faithful and you will be rewarded.

May God bless you all.

Brandon Brown Awards and Achievements

- Citizen of the Year in 2022
- Best HVAC and plumbing company in central VA 7 years straight and counting
- Named to Top 40 under 40 business owner on ACCA Air Conditioners Contractors of America
- Made the 2020 Who's Who book
- Top 3 small businesses with 50 employees or less to work for or do business with
- Talk of the town 5 star company 10 plus years
- Small business of the year 2 times
- Top 3 civic leaders in central VA 2021-2022
- NSBA Leadership Council 2022- Current
- Conquer business coach
- Small business owner of the year 2020-2023
- And now an author

About the Author

Brandon Brown was born and raised in Concord, VA, to Randy and JoAnne Brown. Brandon is now married to his best friend, Dara, and they have two boys, Parker and Dawson. Brandon and Dara run Browns Heating Air & Plumbing since 2006. They love giving back to the community and helping others grow in their business. Brandon also works with a company called Conquer as a business coach, helping other small businesses grow as he did. He gives all thanks and glory to God for his success.

Made in the USA
Columbia, SC
24 October 2024